12.1-23

TON

D0808371

Making Good Habits, Breaking Bad Habits

FOURTEEN NEW BEHAVIOURS THAT WILL ENERGISE YOUR LIFE

JOYCE MEYER

**HODDER &
STOUGHTON**

Unless otherwise noted, Scripture quotations are taken from The Amplified Bible (AMP).
The Amplified Bible, Old Testament,
Copyright © 1965, 1987 by The Zondervan Corporation.
The Amplified New Testament, Copyright © 1954,
1958, 1987 by The Lockman Foundation. Used by Permission.

Scripture quotations marked (NKJV) are taken from the
New King James Version.
Copyright © 1979, 1980, 1982 by Thomas Nelson, Inc., Publishers.

First published in Great Britain in 2013 by Hodder & Stoughton
An Hachette UK company

Published in association with FaithWords, a division of Hachette Book Group USA, Inc.

1

A CIP catalogue record for this title is available from the British Library

ISBN 978 1 444 74993 9
eBook ISBN 978 1 444 74994 6

Printed and bound in the UK by Clays Ltd, St Ives PLC

Hodder & Stoughton policy is to use papers that are natural,
renewable and recyclable products and made from wood grown in
sustainable forests. The logging and manufacturing processes are expected
to conform to the environmental regulations of the country of origin.

Hodder & Stoughton Ltd
338 Euston Road
London NW1 3BH

www.hodderfaith.com

CONTENTS

INTRODUCTION

We all have habits. Some of them are good and some are bad. The good ones benefit us and add joy and power to our lives, while the bad ones do nothing but steal our peace and joy and prevent our success. A habit is something we do without even thinking about it. It is our usual manner of behavior, or a behavior pattern acquired by frequent repetition. I have read that as much as 40 percent of everything we do is done merely from habit.

If you are reading this book it is probably because you have formed a habit of frequent reading. Others who desperately need the information contained in this book won't get it simply because they have not formed a habit of reading. They probably say, "I hate to read." If you repeatedly say you hate a thing, it only makes it harder to do and less enjoyable.

Good habits can be developed, and any bad habit can be broken through repetition. The experts say that a habit can be formed or broken in thirty days, so I am inviting you to give it a try and change your life by changing your habits. At first it may be difficult, but diligence and patience will eventually make you succeed. One of the reasons we don't develop the good habits we say we want is because we live in a culture of instant gratification. We want everything *now* and don't realize that many of the good things we want and need are not attained just because we want them. Good habits come to those who are persistent and refuse to quit.

Vince Lombardi said, "Winning is a habit; unfortunately, so is losing." He also said, "Once you learn to quit, it becomes a habit." Make a decision right now that you can and will be a winner at forming any good habit you want to form and breaking any bad habit that you want to break.

Never start a project with doubt and fear that you won't succeed. Begin this book with the simple belief that you can change. With God's help, you can form good habits and break bad ones. You can become a better person by developing better habits.

Recently, *Real Simple* magazine asked its readers what habits they wanted to break. The list of answers was huge! Among them were:

- Cell phone addiction
- Eavesdropping
- Never finishing projects
- Nail-biting
- Shopping as entertainment
- Cluttering
- Self-criticizing
- Watching too much television
- Hitting the snooze button
- Driving too fast

Now imagine trying to break all those habits all at once. Do you think you'll succeed? I can pretty much assure you that you won't. You'll be too overwhelmed. On top of that, it takes con-centration and effort to break a habit, and the older the habit, the more ingrained it is. So the first key is to choose a single habit that you want to overcome. If you start working to conquer a smaller habit, it will take less time to conquer it than a bigger one. Start small. Your victory will encourage you to tackle another habit, one that's perhaps a bit harder to break. That victory will give you more enthusiasm and resolve to break the next.

> Habit is habit, and not to be flung out of the window by any man, but coaxed downstairs a step at a time.
>
> *Mark Twain*

Make a list of all the habits you want to make and all the ones you want to break. Now **choose one** and use the principles in this book to help you do what you want to do, and stop doing what you don't want to do. If you focus, one at a time, on the habits you want to make, eventually they'll become second nature. If you focus—one at a time—on those you want to break, eventually you will conquer them all. But if you look at them all at once you will probably feel overwhelmed and be defeated before you ever begin. Working toward a change is much easier if we take one thing, one day at a time, and stick with it until we experience breakthrough. Don't ever be discouraged with yourself because you have not arrived at success, but instead be pleased that you are pressing toward it. Discouragement will only zap the strength you need—and have—to eventually succeed.

I must admit that I am very excited for myself as a writer and for you as a reader because I know that we will both benefit from this book. I am looking forward to forming better habits and I pray that you are too. Merely reading this book won't give you the success you desire, but it will give you the tools you need and hopefully ignite in you a passion for change. And passion is like jet fuel: Once you have it, there will be no stopping you!

Making
Good Habits,
Breaking
Bad Habits

CHAPTER
1

The Anatomy of a Habit

Habits are things we learn to do through repetition and eventually do either unconsciously or with very little effort. First we form habits and then they form us. We are what we repeatedly do. Don't be deceived by thinking that you just can't help what you do, because the truth is that you can do or not do anything if you really want to. At least you can do anything that is God's will, and those are the things we will discuss in this book.

I have learned that concentrating on the good things I want and need to do helps me overcome the bad things that I don't want to do. The Bible says in Romans 12:21 that we overcome evil with good. I believe that should be one of our foundation Scriptures for this book and the journey we are embarking on. The other Scripture I want you to remember as you work toward your goals is found in Galatians.

But I say, walk *and* live [habitually] in the [Holy] Spirit [responsive to *and* controlled *and* guided by the Spirit]; then you will certainly not gratify the cravings and desires of the flesh (of human nature without God).

Galatians 5:16

Concentrating on the evil things you are doing will never help you do the good things that you desire to do. This is a very important biblical truth. Good has more power than evil. Darkness is swallowed up in light, and death is overcome by life. Whatever God offers is always more powerful than what Satan desires for us. The devil wants us to have bad habits, but God's desire is that we follow the Holy Spirit and let Him lead us into the good life that Jesus died for us to enjoy. And a good life is a life with good habits.

One of the ingredients of forming good habits and breaking bad ones is focusing on what you want to do and not on what you want to stop doing. For example, if you overeat and want to form balanced, healthy eating habits, don't think about food all the time! Don't read cookbooks that are filled with beautiful, mouthwatering desserts, but instead read a good book on nutrition that will educate you about how to make better choices. Stay busy doing things that will keep your mind off of food.

If you want to form a habit of regular exercise, don't think and talk about how hard it is, but think about the results you will have if you are persistent. Yes, you will have to invest time that you may not think you have to spare, and yes, you will get very sore in the beginning. When I first started working out with a trainer in 2006 at the age of sixty-four, I got so sore that I actually felt as though I was sick. And I stayed sore for what seemed to me like two years. Honestly, I was sore somewhere all the time. Eventually I got to the point where I enjoyed the feeling because I knew that it meant that I was making progress.

If you want to get out of debt, don't think and talk about all the things you won't be able to do and all the things you will have to do without while you are paying off your bills. Instead of thinking of the negative side of your goal, think and talk about how wonderful it will be to be free from the tyranny of over-whelming debt.

We are motivated by reward, so if you will look forward to the reward, you'll have the stamina you need to keep pressing toward your goal. Don't defeat yourself before you even begin by setting your mind on the wrong things. Where the mind goes the person follows, so be sure that your thoughts are on what you want rather than what you don't want.

Repetition

Repetition is the key to forming habits, good or bad. When work-ing toward forming a good habit, you may have to leave notes for yourself to remind you to do the good thing you desire. Ask the Holy Spirit to remind you, too. The Bible says that He will bring all things to our remembrance when we need them (John 14:26).

My daughter Sandra needs words of encouragement. It is her love language, which means she feels loved when people encour-age her. Her husband, Steve, doesn't "speak that language," so in the beginning of their marriage. it didn't occur to him to encourage Sandra verbally. After a few tearful episodes and her telling him several times how important this was to her, he started putting notes on his calendar reminding him to encourage and compliment her. End of problem! Sometimes a simple mechanism such as automatic reminders is the best way to start creating a new habit.

One man shared that he kept a rubber band on his wrist for a year, and every time he caught himself biting his nails, he snapped himself with it to remind him to quit biting his nails. It eventually worked. Some people put a bitter-tasting liquid on their fingernails. When they start to bite them subconsciously, the bad taste reminds them to stop.

The bad habits in our lives are our enemies because they hinder us from being the person we want to be. When an enemy is trying to destroy you, you cannot show that enemy mercy. God was leading the Israelites to possess the land He had promised them, just as He is leading us into the good life He has promised us. Many enemy nations were coming against them, just as the devil is against us. God told the Israelites to utterly destroy the enemy nations and to make no covenants with them and not to show them mercy, and we must do the same thing with the bad habits we have that are stealing our destiny (Deuteronomy 7:1–2). Deal with bad habits relentlessly and without mercy. Find ways to help yourself do the good things that you truly want to do.

Don't fail to realize that bad habits steal the destiny God has preordained for you. Don't think, "Oh, it's just a bad habit, it's not that big a deal." If you think like that, you will more than likely never deal with that habit. Say to yourself instead, "This bad habit is my enemy. It is stealing the quality of life that Jesus wants me to have, and I am not going to permit it to remain in my life."

Theresa had a bad habit of hitting the snooze bar on her alarm too many times, and she was consistently late for work. She had to break this habit or she was likely to lose her job, so she moved the alarm clock across the room to force her to get out of bed to shut it off. She even went a step further by first pulling the sheets and covers up to the top of the mattress to remind herself not to crawl back into bed. In doing these things, Theresa was dealing aggressively not only with her bad habit but also with her enemy.

Rhonda's husband drank several glasses of whole milk each day. She was concerned about his fat and cholesterol intake, so she gradually added skim milk to the whole-milk carton until eventually her husband was drinking all skim milk. He now says that whole milk tastes weird. This shows how we can gradually get accustomed to something that is better for us and not even miss the thing we previously did that wasn't good for us.

Carolyn had a bad habit of eating containers of buttercream frosting. She would sit and watch television while spooning it into her mouth—without cake. In an evening she would consume 3,380 calories of pure sugar. She knew this was a very bad habit and an unhealthy one, so she took serious measures to stop. She asked her husband to throw it in the trash if she brought home a container of frosting from the store. But that didn't work because she would simply dig in the trash and get it out. She finally asked him to empty the container and fill it with dishwashing liquid. She no longer eats containers of frosting.

Reprogram Yourself

It's amazing how powerful your subconscious mind is. Every single time you do something, your subconscious programs it into your brain. The more you do it, the more entrenched the program becomes. I have been amazed at how difficult it is for me to do a new exercise and how much easier it gets each time I do it. My coach told me that it is not because I am too weak to do the new exercise but because my cells have to get accustomed to doing it. Each time I do a new exercise, my cells remember it and it is easier the next time. God has created us in an amazing way, and He has enabled us to be excellent people simply through doing the best things over and over again until they become part of who we are.

I have a bad habit of throwing my makeup brushes into a drawer after I use them. When I put on my makeup the next day, I get frustrated because it seems I can never find the brush I want. So I am in the process of forming a new habit right now. In order to do so, I have had to slow down and keep my mind on what I am doing. Now, as I use the brushes, I take the time to put them where I know they will be the next day. I have only been at it about three days, but by the end of three or four weeks it will be a habit and I won't have to put out the same effort to remember it that I do now. I think a lot of our bad habits are simply the result of being in too big a hurry to do a thing right to start with.

Some people never pay attention to what they are doing, so they almost never know where anything is when they need it. This type of disorganization causes a lot of frustration, stress, and loss of precious time. Through repetition, you can become organized in any area you need to. Remember, though difficult at first, it will get easier as time goes by. Slow down, breathe, and actually take the time to think about what you are doing.

Charles Dickens said, "I could never have done what I have done without the habits of punctuality, order, and diligence, without the determination to concentrate myself on one subject at a time." God had given him a tremendous gift of storytelling, but he still had to form good habits of concentration, order, and diligence to be a good steward of his talent.

Many people are talented but don't bother to form good habits. They won't discipline themselves to do what they know they should do, but instead they wait to be moved by some outside force. This is called passivity, and it is a huge open door for the devil. If we are not actively doing what is right, it becomes very easy for the devil to get us to do what is wrong.

Be Active

God's Word encourages us to be active, and by being active we shut the door to laziness, procrastination, and passivity. Remember, if we do the right thing, there will be no room for the wrong thing. Don't merely focus on breaking all of your bad habits but instead use your energy to actively form good habits. You will soon find there is no room in your life for the bad ones.

Don't wait to "feel" like doing a thing to do it. Live by decision, not emotion. I have learned by experience that the more I sit around and do nothing, the more I want to sit around and do nothing, but if I get up and get moving, then energy begins to flow. Activity is like flipping on a light switch. The power is there all the time, but it is not ignited until you flip the switch. We always have the ability to be active, but no energy flows until we actually get moving.

There are mornings when I feel sluggish and as if I could just sit in a chair all day, but I have learned that after my exercise routine, I feel energetic, and that helps to motivate me to do it. If you feel sluggish, try taking a walk or doing some other kind of activity that will get your blood circulating. Don't wait to feel like it; just do it. You are more powerful than you may realize. God has given you free will, and that means you can decide to do what is right and nothing can stop you. When we decide in favor of God's ways, He always joins forces with us for assured victory.

As we leave this chapter, choose a habit you want to form and begin putting these principles into practice. Be patient with yourself. It takes time to create habits, and you may not succeed every day. If you realize you have failed, don't waste time being discouraged; just pick up where you left off and begin again. Be kind to yourself, because beating yourself up for every mistake is another bad habit that needs to be broken.

CHAPTER
2

Get Started Now!

A journey of a thousand miles
begins with one step.

Lao-Tzu

The biggest thief of success is procrastination. We can think about doing the right thing, plan to do it, and talk about doing it, but nothing changes in our lives until we start consistently doing what we need to do. Perhaps you have so many bad habits that you feel overwhelmed, and you are not even sure that you want to read the rest of this book. You would like to *have* change, but you're not sure you want to *change*. Someone said, "Bad habits are like a comfortable bed, easy to get into, but hard to get out of." Bruce Barton said, "What a curious phenomenon it is that you can get men to die for the liberty of the world who will not make the little sacrifice that is needed to free themselves from their own individual bondage."

Are you willing to sacrifice and do the more difficult thing now in order to enjoy a life of freedom later on? The irony is that we are often unwilling to suffer for a short while just to do what needs to be done; then we end up with continual misery, dread, guilt, and the penalties of having put off something that would have taken a few minutes or a few hours to do. In other words, by putting off the "pain" of doing something hard, we often spend much *more* time avoiding it than it would take to just do it.

To me nothing feels better than knowing that I am doing my best, making the best choices I can make, and consistently making progress toward the best life that God has for me. Being mediocre does not feel good to me, and I doubt that it feels good to you either. You may have gotten used to it and forgotten that there is something better, but this is a wake-up call to arise and be all you can be. The best time to get started is now!

We can become very addicted to our little habits and find it difficult to give them up even if they are harming us. We all have good and bad habits, but Benjamin Franklin said, "Your net worth to the world is usually determined by what remains after your bad habits are subtracted from your good ones." Get started right now forming all the good habits you can. Soon they will outnumber the bad ones, and your value to yourself, your family, your friends and society will increase exponentially.

Defeat Procrastination

The way to get started is to quit talking and begin doing.

Walt Disney

Procrastination is very deceptive. It makes us complacent by telling us that we are *going* to do the right thing. It justifies inactivity. I once heard a story about three demons who were graduating from their course on how to deceive people in the world and prevent them from knowing God. Satan was questioning each demon, and he asked each one how he would deceive people. The first one answered that he would tell people there was no God. Satan answered, "You won't deceive many because most people down deep inside of them do believe God exists even if they have not chosen to follow Him." The second demon said he would tell people that heaven and hell didn't really exist. Satan said, "You will deceive a few more than your coworker, but you won't get many souls either." The third demon said that he would tell people that there was no hurry, and they could put off the decision to follow God until another time. Satan got excited and said loudly, "You will reap many souls for the kingdom of darkness by simply telling them to make the decision later." I have never forgotten this story even though I heard it approximately twenty years ago.

Procrastination is a thief. It steals our time, our potential, our self-esteem, our peace of mind. It is like a lullaby that whispers, "Go to sleep; everything will be fine." But everything will not be fine if we put off doing what we need to do. And the task isn't going to get done by itself! It's not going anywhere. Procrastination is very deceptive, and we can only conquer it by becoming what I call a "now" person. Be aggressive when you know you need to do something. Don't put it off and keep putting it off... just do it!

I am sitting in my bedroom this morning working on this

book. A few minutes ago I looked at my bed, which was still unmade. I got up to get something, and as I passed by the bed I thought about making it and then thought, "Oh, I will do it later." I could have done that, but I know myself well enough to know that I would have found looking at the messed-up bed unpleasant throughout the day. I recognize the importance of doing what I need to do right away, so I defeated procrastination by simply taking a few minutes to make the bed. Now I feel better about myself and about the way the room looks and I can get back to work.

When we put things off, they aggravate us. We may not even be consciously aware of it, but unfinished projects pressure us. If you walk through your home and see dishes in the sink, laundry on the floor, trash cans filled to the brim, beds unmade, every countertop piled high with mail that needs to be sorted, I feel certain that it pressures you in some way. You may even get grouchy and start an argument with someone else in the house just because you feel overwhelmed. When we find fault with someone else it diverts our attention from how we feel about ourselves. Procrastination never makes us feel good.

If the grass needs to be cut, the weeds need to be pulled, the car needs to be washed and the oil needs to be changed, and the garage is a disorganized mess, it pressures you. You can complain about the mess or you can stop procrastinating and take action—one item at a time—to bring order to your home. God is certainly a God of order and organization. Some of the details recorded in the Bible about the building of the Ark and the Temple are just amazing to me. God made sure that everything was done in the most orderly and best way possible. Chaos makes us feel confused, and God is not the author of confusion but of order and peace (1 Corinthians 14:33).

I want to share with you the story of a woman who had only one bad habit. Ellen was a warm, generous woman who was extremely intelligent and talented. Her husband, children, and grandchildren adored her. Her colleagues at the elementary school where she taught marveled at her rapport with the young children in her classes and her ability to impart to them the love of learning. She was close to her parents and treasured her many friendships. Ellen was so busy keeping up with all these things that she found herself at home very little, and when she was at home, she was exhausted.

One day after work she collected the mail and just put it in a pile on her desk. She didn't feel like dealing with it right then; it could wait until the next day. She needed to complete her students' grades for the year, which would require a few hours. But she had two weeks before those were due, so she decided to enjoy some well-earned downtime and watch a movie instead. Ellen's grandchildren were going to arrive for a weeklong visit during spring break, which would start in a few days. The house was a mess, but she still had the weekend to clean and prepare for the visit. Ellen had promised her husband that she would renew the registrations on their cars, which were due in a few days. The final reminder was in the pile of mail she'd left on the desk.

The next night Ellen came home as tired as she'd been the evening before. So she threw the day's mail on the desk and headed into the kitchen to prepare dinner. After the meal, the evening vanished as she returned phone calls from friends and watched a little TV. One day turned into another...and all the while small things piled up waiting for Ellen's attention.

There wasn't any one big reason for the fact that Ellen's life became harder and more unhapppy. It was just the culmination of a lot of little tasks and responsibilities that Ellen had put off. Tasks like paying the bills on time, tidying up the house, handing in her students' grades accurately and on time—none of them major.

Maybe you can guess how this story is going to end. Bills piled up unpaid. There was enough money in the couple's bank account to pay them—Ellen just disliked the chore of bill paying. Eventually penalties accrued and ultimately most of the cards were revoked for delinquency. Ellen was a great teacher, but her paperwork was always late. When her school had to trim the faculty, Ellen was the person who was laid off. Remember that car registration that Ellen was supposed to renew? She forgot. As a result, she and her husband couldn't take their grandchildren on the getaway they'd planned . . . the suspended registrations kept the cars in the driveway that week.

Ellen only had one bad habit. But that single habit of procrastination created so many small problems that they eventually added up to big problems.

You can form the habit of being a "now" person, one who does what needs to be done as soon as you can. All truly successful people have this habit. We don't become successful by putting things off. Here are a few quotes on procrastination that I think are particularly helpful:

- "Procrastination is like a credit card, it is a lot of fun until you get the bill." Christopher Parker

- "There are so many things that we wish we had done yesterday, and so few that we feel like doing today." Mignon McLaughlin
- "If you have goals and procrastination, you have nothing. If you have goals and you take action, you will have anything you want." Thomas J. Vilord
- "Procrastination is the kidnapper of souls, and the recruiting-officer of Hell." Edward Irving
- "Procrastination is the seed of self-destruction." Matthew Burton
- "When there is a hill to climb don't think that waiting will make it smaller." Author Unknown
- "Procrastination is suicide on the installment plan." Author Unknown

Faith Lives in the Present

As believers in Jesus Christ, we learn that we receive everything we need from God through faith. Faith is now! It is trusting now that God will take care of yesterday and tomorrow. We are justified and made right with God through faith alone, yet the apostle James tells us that faith without works is dead.

So also faith, if it does not have works (deeds and actions of obedience to back it up), by itself is destitute of power (inoperative, dead).

James 2:17

There are probably thousands upon thousands of people who consider themselves to be great people of faith, and yet they procrastinate all the time. Procrastination is not faith, because true faith demands action. It is true that faith sometimes waits for God to work, but most of the time it must take action to be obedient when God speaks.

We need not wait for some special word from God telling us what to do. In the Bible, God has already given us most of the direction we will need in our lives. When I noticed my unmade bed, I did not need a special word from God to know that the best thing to do would be to make it up. The only thing left to do was obey.

I realize that some of you may have serious bad habits, and you may be thinking that my example of an unmade bed is rather unimportant. However, I am of the opinion that if we are willing to obey and take action in the smallest detail, we will have fewer problems with the bigger projects in life.

Let me offer some help by using examples from my life where procrastinating caused huge problems. For example, I had back pain for many years, but it was not so serious that I couldn't work through it each day. Friends and family told me often that I needed to see a doctor or a chiropractor, but I procrastinated year after year. Finally one morning I was unable to walk when I got out of bed and had no choice but to make an emergency appointment with a chiropractor. My back was inflamed, and I had some disk degeneration. Pain is a signal that something is wrong and needs attention, and when we ignore it, we only complicate the problem. If I had taken care of my back and gotten some professional advice when the pain first surfaced, I could possibly have saved myself a great deal of pain and hundreds of hours of time spent on doctor visits over the years. Remember, procrastination is fun until reality sets in.

I remember a dentist telling me once, "We need you to start coming in for your regular cleaning and checkups so you can stop needing emergency appointments because you have a tooth-ache." He reminded me that the only time he saw me was when I had had an emergency, which wasn't fair to him because my emergency put pressure on his already full schedule. Not only that, but my procrastinating exacted a high price from me. After all, it's less painful—and less expensive—to have a cavity filled than to have oral surgery.

My excuse for procrastinating was that I was busy. Does that sound familiar? When we refuse to use our time to do the things we need to do, we always end up losing time taking care of the emergencies and messes we created through procrastinating.

I hope you have chosen one good habit that you want to make and one bad habit that you want to break. NOW is the time to get started! While I am writing this book we are in the Christmas and New Year season, and I have heard several people declare what they are going to do as soon as the holidays are over. They are going to lose weight, begin an exercise program, organize their lives, and other similar things. A few of them may follow through, but honestly I already know that most of them won't. They are procrastinators, and people who procrastinate today will find a reason to do so tomorrow also.

I started my current workout regimen on December 23, 2006, and God has given me the grace to continue doing it. My trainer said I had to begin the program with twenty-one days of no sugar, and he gave me a specific diet I was to follow that was designed to shock my body and reset my metabolism. I recall people asking me why in the world I started such a program the day before Christmas Eve. I did it because I thought if I could do it during the most luscious eating times of the year, then surely I could do it the rest of the time. It is not wise to wait until a time that you feel will be convenient to begin any task. Great character is not developed through ease and convenience but through doing NOW what needs to be done no matter how difficult it is.

Get Excited About Conquering Projects

All those who have received Jesus as their Savior and Lord have His Spirit in them, and His Spirit is one of a Conqueror. Jesus is a mighty warrior, and He has not called us to be fainting saints. Don't dread anything, but instead conquer it. The longer we put something off and think about it, the more we turn what is actually a molehill into a mountain. When we are people of action, we don't give the devil time to exaggerate the reality of what we are facing. Don't dread making and breaking habits, but be excited about the challenge in front of you. I honestly don't want to live without goals, and when I accomplish one, I look forward to the next one. I don't always like the work involved, but I love, love, love the results and the feeling of conquering and accomplishment. I believe you will too. I have heard people say, "I am just a procrastinator," as if that were their identity. We are children of God, joint heirs with Christ, filled with the Holy Spirit, anointed by God, gifted, talented, and able to do whatever we need to do in life through Christ (Philippians 4:13).

If you have the small opinion of yourself that you are merely a procrastinator, you are pitiful indeed. I encourage you to get a new attitude, one of a warrior and a conqueror. Look forward to climbing mountains. Caleb asked for a mountain when he was eighty years old! (See Numbers 13.) Why not? He knew that as long as God was with him, he could do great things.

Congratulations! You are still reading, and that means you are on your way to making good habits and breaking bad ones. Choose something and begin today. Stick with it until you have victory, and then choose another and repeat the process. Don't stop until you have developed the habits you want to have.

3

Behavior 1: The God Habit

And He came out and went, as was His habit,
to the Mount of Olives, and the disciples also
followed Him.

Luke 22:39

Jesus did not have a habit of going to the Mount of Olives because He liked mountain climbing. He went there to pray. Notice that it was His habit to go there. You will find throughout Scripture that all of the great men and women of God had similar habits. They all knew the vital importance of spending time with God. The Bible says that Enoch habitually walked with God "and he was not, for God took him" (Genesis 5:24). Here is a man who developed such an intimate relationship with God that the world could no longer hold him. Enoch had developed what I will reverently call the God habit.

Jesus was about to enter one of the most difficult times of His life on earth. The time for His suffering and death was near. He knew that He needed strength and He knew where to get it. It was His habit, His automatic response not only in times of tribulation but at all times to spend time with His heavenly Father. If you are like I once was and only go to God when you have an emergency, then I can tell you that while He's not mad at you, God is not pleased. How would you like it if your friends or children only came to see you or spoke to you when they needed your help? You wouldn't like it at all, and God doesn't like it either.

The God habit is the first one that I want to address, because without the habit of spending time with God in prayer and studying His Word, we will be unable to develop any other good habits, and bad habits will overtake us and rule our lives. Seeking and spending time with Him is our most vital need.

> You have said, Seek My face [inquire for and require My presence as your vital need]. My heart says to You, Your face (Your presence), Lord, will I seek, inquire for, *and* require [of necessity and on the authority of Your Word]
>
> *Psalm 27:8*

God's help and presence in our lives is vital. He is the Author of all true success and everything that is good, and without Him we can do nothing of true value. Are you taking time to ask for God's help before you begin your day, make decisions, or undertake any endeavor? Develop the habit of acknowledging God in all your ways and then He will direct your steps (Proverbs 3:6).

We are usually accustomed to making our own decisions and trying in our own strength to make the things happen that we want to take place, but that is truly a bad habit that needs to be broken. The habit of acknowledging God in all your ways may be the first and most important habit that you should develop.

I have known a few people with extremely strong willpower who have developed some good habits through discipline, but that does not mean they are truly successful. I have a strong will and it has been a benefit to me, but I have learned that our will-power takes us only so far, and we all discover sooner or later that we need God.

Time Management

We took a short survey at our office of some of the habits people want to make and break, and right on top of the list was "I want to form a habit of spending more time with God." We all have the same amount of time each day, but some people regularly find time to spend with God, and others never do. Saying that we don't have time to spend with God is simply an excuse. The truth is that if we spend time with God, He will multiply what we have left—like the little boy with the loaves and fish (John 6)—and we will end up with more time than we would have had by leaving God out of our schedule.

The truth is that at this moment, you are as close to God as you want to be. What we sow we will reap, and if we want a bigger harvest, then we simply need to sow more seed. If we want a closer relationship with God, then we need to spend more time with Him.

My granddaughter, who is ten years old, recently asked me how she could spend more time with God, since she is so busy with school and all her activities. I thought that was really cute. She thinks she is busy now; I can't imagine what she will think as life really gets into a full roar for her. She has a very bad habit of being cranky in the mornings and wants to get over it, so I told her that the best thing to do is get out of bed and spend the first five minutes with God. I thought five minutes would be a good place for her to begin, and if you have not formed this very important habit, it might be a good place for you to begin too. A small beginning is better than no beginning at all.

We need God, and we are no good without Him. He said, "If you seek me, you will find me" (Jeremiah 29:13). He is waiting for us to call on Him and talk to Him about every aspect of our lives. He wants to hear us say that we need Him, love Him, and that He is a vital necessity in our lives.

Put First Things First

How can we ever hope to have order in our lives if we don't know how to put the most important thing ahead of other things? I tried for many years to work God into my schedule, and the devil made sure I never found the time. Each night I felt guilty because once again I had failed to spend time with God, and I always promised myself that the next day would be different, but sadly it was a repeat of the day before. I had good intentions, but procrastination got the best of me. I was always going to spend time with God after the one more thing I needed to take care of.

Not much was working right in my life or ministry. I was frustrated most of the time about one thing or another and felt that any progress was made at a snail's pace. I am grateful to say that God finally got through to me, and I have learned how to work my schedule around God, who is first, rather than trying to work Him into my schedule.

Jesus said it plainly:

Come to Me, all you who labor and are heavy-laden and overburdened, and I will cause you to rest. [I will ease and relieve and refresh your souls.]

Matthew 11:28

The answer to my problem was simple, and so is yours. Come to Jesus! Take time first thing each day to communicate with your Father in heaven who loves you and wants to be involved in all that you do. You may not have a lot of time to spend with God in the morning, but to give Him no time at all is tragic and insulting. We should give Him lots of time each day, but when you do it is up to you. It may be at lunch, or in the evening, but please don't ignore Him. My lifestyle is such that I can make my own schedule, so I spend the first portion of each morning with God, but it is not my place to tell you how you should structure your spiritual life. I will say that I believe and can prove biblically that to seek Him early in the morning is wise. Even if you can't spend a lot of time with God as soon as you get up, at least take time to say,

"Good morning, Lord. I love You. Thank You for everything You do for me. I need You. Please help me today."

> In the morning You hear my voice, O Lord; in the morning
> I prepare [a prayer, a sacrifice] for You and watch and wait
> [for You to speak to my heart].
>
> *Psalm 5:3*

Mary Magdalene was the first one to see Jesus after His resurrection, but she also was the one who came to the tomb **early** (John 20:1). The other disciples stayed in bed, but Mary arose early and went to look for her Lord.

I need and receive a lot of help from God, and receiving the following Scripture as direction for my life has helped me in amazing ways.

> God is in the midst of her, she shall not be moved; God will
> help her right early [at the dawn of the morning].
>
> *Psalm 46:5*

I could quote several other Scriptures to make my point, but I think you understand what I am trying to say. *The earlier, the better* should be our motto as far as connecting with God is concerned. In fact, *the earlier, the better* is a principle that should be applied to many areas in our lives.

Another piece of wisdom that has been helpful to me is *don't do nothing simply because you can't do a lot.* If you want to form a habit of spending time with God, then start small and progress.

Sometimes we are defeated because we try to begin where we should be finishing, or we try to do what someone is doing who has had forty years' experience with God.

I don't believe God counts the minutes and hours we spend with Him, and I personally gave that belief up long ago. If I spend a lot of time with God and keep a mental record of it, I may be in danger of pride, and if I spend what I think is not enough, then I will feel guilty, and neither pride nor guilt are going to help me in my walk with God. I just spend as much time as I feel I need each day. To me it is like eating. I stop when I get full, and sometimes I need to eat more than at other times.

I don't want to give you a program to follow; I only want to encourage you to form a habit of putting God first in everything you do. If you will seek first His Kingdom, He will add all of the other things that you need (Matthew 6:33).

Get the God Habit

I have the God habit, and I can tell you that it is the most important habit of all. God's Word teaches us that we can do nothing without Him; therefore, it makes sense to make it a priority to form the habit of putting Him first. Perhaps you are at the point in your life where you are ready to form the habit, and if so, then you are at a good place. As a matter of fact, I want to encourage you to go all the way and get addicted to God. Put Him before all other things. Be totally unable to do without His guidance and presence in your life. If I tried to start a day without seeking God,

I would feel like some people do if they try to start a day without sugar or caffeine. I am addicted! I wasted many years not putting God first, and as I look back, they were the most miserable years of my life. God and good things go together, so if we want to have a good life that we can enjoy, we must have the God habit.

Under the Old Testament law, when the Israelites went into battle, they had to make sure that the Ark of the Covenant that carried God's presence always went first. Because of that, the Israelites won most of their battles. There was a time, however, when David tried to put the Ark on a new cart and have some men drive oxen pulling the Ark behind them. The outcome was disastrous (1 Chronicles 13). The message here is plain: *If God is first, then we will be winners in life, but if He isn't, there is no reason to expect anything to work out right.* Billy Graham said, "Heaven is full of answers for which nobody ever bothered to ask." Start asking and receiving, that your joy may be full (John 16:24).

Thankfully we have now become the Ark, or the house of God. He lives inside the hearts of those who believe in Jesus. We don't have to go find Him, because He is always near. We just need to pay attention to Him. I wouldn't like it if I lived in someone's house and they ignored me most of the time, and I don't think God likes it either.

It is amazing to me that God has chosen to make our hearts His home. It is a beautiful thought and a tremendous privilege, so we should develop the habit of regular conversation with Him. If you overspiritualize prayer, you are in danger of not doing it. Remember, prayer is simply talking to God, worshipping and praising Him, and being thankful at all times.

The Word Habit

It is impossible to develop the God habit if we don't have the Word habit. God and His Word are always connected. Jesus is the Word made flesh who came to dwell among us.

> And the Word (Christ) became flesh (human, incarnate) and tabernacled (fixed His tent of flesh, lived awhile) among us; and we [actually] saw His glory...
>
> *John 1:14*

We cannot know God apart from His Word, so we must be committed to studying it, meditating on it, and making it the basis of all that we do. God's Word is truth and it shows us the way we are to live. Psalm 119 contains 176 verses that all teach us the vital importance of hearing, meditating on, loving, receiving, and obeying God's Word.

> Your word have I laid up in my heart, that I might not sin against You.
>
> *Psalm 119:11*

> This I have had [as the gift of Your grace and as my reward]: that I have kept Your precepts [hearing, receiving, loving, and obeying them].
>
> *Psalm 119:56*

Oh, how love I Your law! It is my meditation all the day.

Psalm 119:97

Studying God's Word can become a habit in the same way that we form all other good habits. We begin with some effort and keep at it until doing it becomes a regular habit in our life. It develops into something that is done habitually with little or no effort. You might begin with a commitment to read God's Word (the Bible) fifteen minutes each day. Do that for two weeks and then increase it a couple of minutes each week until you reach your desired goal. After a while you will not need to have a set amount of time that you are committed to because you will probably have to discipline yourself to stop reading so you can tend to other things.

I also suggest that you keep a journal or computer with you, and as you read or after you are finished, make a note of the thing or things you feel you learned through your reading. This helps us to retain the knowledge we have received. You can benefit even more if you think about (meditate on) what you have learned throughout the day, or talk to someone else about it. You can also speak what you have learned out loud during times when you are alone just to help you deepen your awareness and remembrance of it.

With my lips have I declared *and* recounted all the ordinances of Your mouth.

Psalm 119:13

Start with portions of the Bible that you can readily understand. Most people feel that the New Testament is easier to understand than some portions of the Old Testament. Frequently the Gospel of John is suggested as a good place to begin. Psalms and Proverbs are also very practical and easily understood so they are also a good place to begin. Eventually you can progress to being able to read and understand all of God's Word.

Through knowledge of God's Word you will learn to know Him. You will learn His character and ways, and you will learn how much He loves you and what a wonderful plan He has for your life.

Once you have God's Word deeply implanted in your heart, it will give you direction when you find yourself in situations where wisdom is needed.

I attended church and believed that Christ was my Savior for many years before I became committed to diligently studying God's Word. I can honestly say that during those years I had very little if any spiritual growth. I was generally unhappy, frustrated, and did not display behavior that would be proper for someone calling themselves a Christian. God's Word is our spiritual food and without it we cannot grow and become strong in Him.

Start now developing the Word habit and let it be one of the most important parts of your God habit!

Beware of the "Religious Compartment"

Don't divide your life into sacred and secular compartments. You can't have a compartment where you keep God and then run the rest of your life yourself. For many years I had a "religious compartment." I went to church on Sunday. Sometimes I read one chapter of the Bible in the evening out of obligation and then said a very short and often meaningless prayer. It is no wonder that my life was like a train wreck. As I have already said, I was an unhappy, miserable, frustrated, unfulfilled Christian. Yes, I said I was a Christian! I believed in and had received Jesus as my Savior. I understood salvation by grace alone and I was truly sorry for my sins. My problem was that I only invited God into my life on Sunday morning and in serious emergencies. I did not have the Word habit or the God habit. I was sad, but He was probably sadder because He had to watch me be miserable while His help was available for the asking. I was miserable because I wasn't giving God access to my whole life. When I did, everything in my life changed for the better.

"You do not have, because you do not ask" (James 4:2). Start talking to God about everything you do. Invite Him into your activities, and if what you're doing and where you're going aren't proper places for God, then stop!

Now you may be putting on the brakes because you know that you may have to make some lifestyle changes if you do that. But those things you may want to hang on to are the things that are stealing your peace and joy anyway, so say good-bye to them and get on with God's plan for your life.

If you will develop the habit of putting God first in all things and inviting Him into everything you do, a lot of your bad habits will be taken care of by the forming of this one good habit.

The more time we spend with Jesus, the more we become like Him. The Bible says that as we study the Word of God, we are transformed into His image, from one degree of glory to another (2 Corinthians 3:18). We see the law of gradual growth in operation in this Scripture. If we are diligent in seeking Him, slowly and surely we become better people.

Prayer doesn't just change things, it also changes us. Prayer is not an obligation, it is a privilege. Spending time with God is habit forming, so get started today!

CHAPTER
4

Breaking Bad Habits

I suspect you bought this book because you have bad habits that you want to break. Perhaps you have tried over and over again and yet have failed, and you are hoping that I have the formula for your success. I do believe I can offer some good advice, but the first thing you must do is ask yourself how serious you are about breaking the habit you want to conquer. I don't have a three-step magic formula that will change you overnight. But I can promise you that you don't have to be in bondage to anything if you truly want to be free.

I want to start this chapter by being honest. Breaking bad habits takes a strong commitment, an investment of time, a lot of hard work, and a willingness to be uncomfortable while you are transitioning from bondage to freedom. If you are not willing to do that, then I doubt that I can help you. Breaking a bad habit can be like breaking up with a bad boyfriend who is abusing us. We know breaking up with him is the right thing to do, but we may miss him even though being with him means being hurt. We must learn to follow the wisdom of God and do what we know will be good for us in the long term and not follow the thing that makes us feel good physically or emotionally for the moment.

Breaking up with bad habits is certainly not easy, but with God's help we can do it.

One of the problems we face in society today is that we have too much ease, and now we are addicted to it. We tend to want everything to be easy, but God has anointed and equipped us for hard things. We can do all things through Christ. He is our strength. The truth is that if a thing costs us nothing, it is rarely very valuable to us. If breaking a bad habit could take place without any commitment or effort on our part, our freedom would not even be valuable enough for us to try to keep it.

There are some very specific steps I believe you should take as you work toward breaking a bad habit. First, be careful how you talk about the habit you are trying to break. From the beginning of your journey toward freedom I am asking you not to say, "This is just too hard; I am not sure I can do it." The more you say it is hard, the harder it will be. Don't go out with friends and talk about how you are trying to break such and such bad habit and how hard it is. Actually, it is my opinion that you would be better off not to talk about it much at all. Keep your goal between you and God and possibly one or two other trusted friends or family members who you want to pray for you and to encourage you. I want to reemphasize this point just to make sure that you don't read over it too quickly and miss it. Make a commitment not to say, "This is so hard; I am not sure I can do it." Say something that will help you, not something that will hinder you. Say, "I can do this with God's help."

Jesus did a hard thing by sacrificing His life for us, and He didn't ever say, "This is just too hard." He did it through prayer, constantly leaning on God, and having a strong commitment to doing the will of God. He, for the joy of obtaining the prize that was set before Him, endured the cross (Hebrews 12:2b). As you begin your journey of breaking bad habits, keep the reward that you will receive in mind. We are motivated by reward, and God is certainly the Rewarder of those who are diligent. When you are weary of doing battle with your wrong desires, think of how wonderful it will be when the bad habit is broken and a good one has taken its place.

The number of bad habits we could talk about is endless, and no matter how many I mention I might miss yours, but the answer to them all is the same. Perhaps you want to quit smoking cigarettes, or overeating, or being critical of others. You may even be dealing with a more serious addiction such as alcoholism, gambling, drug addiction, pornography, or an eating disorder. The name of the addiction is not the important thing. The important thing is for you to know that God loves you unconditionally and Jesus came to undo the works of the devil, to set captives free, and to give us a life that we can enjoy.

All things are possible with God, so whether your bad habit is eating too much sugar or drug addiction, God is able and willing to set you free. I realize that breaking a habit of drinking eight cans of soda a day is not going to be as difficult as breaking an addiction to drugs. The problems are not the same, but God is the same, and He has enough strength to meet whatever your need may be.

Believe

If you want to break a bad habit, you must believe that it's possible. If you try to conquer it while your thoughts and words are filled with doubt and unbelief, you are not likely to experience victory. Even if you have tried a thousand times previously and have never been successful, believe that this time will be different.

Jesus told His disciples that if they would only believe they would see the glory of God (John 11:40). Even if you have days when you're not very successful, keep believing. I think it makes the devil furious when we keep saying, "I believe that God is working and I am free."

Believe God's Word more than you believe how you feel, and learn to say what God says about you and your life. God's Word says that we are dead to sin and that our relationship with it is broken (Romans 6:2) and that we are alive to God, living in unbroken fellowship with Him (Romans 6:11). That means that, spiritually speaking, you are already free from all bad habits, and you just need to believe it and start applying the freedom that Jesus purchased for you with His death and resurrection. We may not feel that way, but that is what God's Word says. It further says that we are to consider (think) ourselves dead to sin and our relationship with it broken (Romans 6:11). How do you think of yourself? Do you always see yourself as someone who is in bondage and a slave to bad habits, or will you take a step in faith and believe you are free?

How you think about the problem you have or the bad habit

you want to break is very important, because our thoughts fuel our actions. You can control your thoughts and should never think that any bad habit is beyond being eliminated from your life. Keep thinking, "I can do this with God's help." Remember, the experts say it takes thirty days to make or break a habit, and if you take it one day at a time it won't seem so difficult.

I realize this principle of believing before seeing may not make any sense at all to your mind, but it is God's formula for success. In the world we are only willing to believe after we see and have proof, but in God's Kingdom we believe first by faith without any natural evidence and then we see the result. Believe first, and then experience freedom. Believe God's Word and results will come.

So far, the things I am urging you to do are:

1. Start every day with God—ask Him for strength and guidance early each day.
2. Be very committed and ready to suffer for a season if necessary.
3. Be careful what you say about the habit.
4. Think positive, faith-filled thoughts about your journey.
5. Believe even when you have not yet seen results.

What Provokes You?

Examine yourself and learn what provokes you to do the behavior you want to be free from. Does stress or some other negative emotion cause you to turn to your bad habit? Do you do it when you are bored? Do you do it when you are lonely? Do you do it every morning? For example, you might never be tempted to eat ice cream and popcorn at 10 a.m., but you are tempted to do it every evening when you watch television. Is your bad habit connected to some other activity that you do? My daughter Laura loves Diet Pepsi. For the most part she has stopped drinking it, but I have noticed that it's when she is frustrated or extremely tired that she says emphatically, "Today I am having a Diet Pepsi!" It is her comfort food. Drinking an occasional Diet Pepsi may not be a problem, but if your habit is to gamble or take drugs when you feel frustrated or stressed, then it is a more urgent matter. Ask God to show you if there is a connection between your habit and other things. Sometimes understanding why we do something is the doorway to freedom.

See if you can find a pattern, and if you do, it may help you avoid the habit by avoiding the thing that triggers it. At the very least, understanding the connection may help you be more prepared to resist the temptation. If you tend to overeat when you're bored, you can either not let yourself get bored or you can find another healthier habit to fill your time than eating excessively. If you shop when you're unhappy as a way of comforting yourself emotionally, then recognizing the pattern can help you find a more biblical way of dealing with your unhappiness.

Focus

I already mentioned that it is best to work on one habit at a time, but I need to stress that point. We are all tempted to try to fix everything that is wrong overnight, but that is impossible. Any bad habits you have were developed one at a time, and they will be broken one at a time. Focus is vital. It allows us to direct all of our energies and power toward one thing, rather than divide them up between several things. Impatience urges us to conquer them all, but success comes through faith and patience. Let's say you have located three bad habits that you seriously want to be free from. If each one takes only thirty days, then in ninety days you will be free from them all, or at least well on your way. Remember, habits are formed through repetition, and they will be broken through repetition. If we repeatedly do a thing, it soon becomes part of who we are and is done unconsciously, as a habit. If we repeatedly do *not* do a thing, then it will fade away, and at some point it will no longer be part of who we are.

People who are overweight need to focus on what they are eating. I have noticed that people who overeat tend to eat mindlessly. If they walk past a fellow employee's desk and a dish of candy is sitting there for all to share, they will pop one in their mouth unconsciously, out of habit. I was overweight in my teenage and young adult years, and since then I have developed many good eating habits, one of which is to never eat anything without realizing what I am eating and approximately how many calories it has. I can eat anything if I really want it, but I have to realize I ate it and take it into account with the rest of what I will eat that day.

Most people who are overweight eat many things throughout the day that they don't even remember eating at all; then they are frustrated because they feel they just don't eat enough to weigh as much as they do. If you have a problem in this area, then I suggest that you write down everything you put into your mouth for about a week. That may give you a reality check. It is easy for us to deceive ourselves unless we take the time to truly pay attention to what we are doing. If you want to break the habit of overeating, you will have to focus on it for at least thirty days. I am sure you will find several things you can do without that will make a difference in your weight. I know of a woman who simply gave up drinking a large glass of milk every night before she went to bed. Over a period of a year she lost fifteen pounds.

If you want to break the bad habit of disorganization, you will need to focus on keeping your surroundings neat and tidy. Several times a day, purposely take a look at your space (your home, your desk, automobile, etc.). If it has gotten messy or cluttered, take a few minutes to tidy it up. Develop the habit of putting things back where they belong right away. A good phrase to remember is "Put it away right away."

Priscilla was always losing her keys. This sounds small, but it led to other habits—like always being late for appointments. Why? Because she was searching for her keys when she should have already left her house. Finally she placed a decorative dish right by the front door and made it a point to put her keys in the dish as soon as she walked in the house. It was easy, and it solved two problems at once. Keeping up with things regularly is much better than letting them pile up until they are overwhelming. Stick with this one thing until you have victory and then you can go on to something else, while continuing to maintain the victory you have already gained.

One thing that helps us focus is to keep something in front of us that reminds us of what we need to do or not do. You are more likely to drink a lot of water if you keep water with you all the time. Write yourself notes and put them in places where you have to see them. If you are trying to break the bad habit of being late, keep a clock in front of you, or set an alarm to remind you when you need to start preparing to leave your home.

We can also focus by keeping certain things away from us. One woman who wanted to quit smoking removed all of the ashtrays and lighters from her house. If you want to stop watching so much TV, take the remote out of the room. You may get so tired of changing channels that you'll decide to do something else. And even if you don't, at least you'll get some exercise. Candy dishes have other uses than holding sweets; you can fill them with unshelled nuts or potpourri.

Finally, don't be angry with yourself because you don't just remember to do all the good things you should do. Don't feel foolish if you have to leave a note for yourself to remind you to do something. It is better to do that than to not do what you should be doing. Develop all the systems you need to help you focus on what you want to accomplish.

Get Out of the Rut!

Sometimes it can help break a bad habit if we realize that it will be dangerous or harmful to continue it. I always had difficulty forming a habit of flossing my teeth daily, even though several dentists over the years had urged me to do so. The truth was that I just didn't want to take the time to do it, and I thought my teeth were okay. I was busy, but eventually I spent the time anyway. This year I had about twenty dentist appointments. I had an abscessed tooth and a total of seventeen teeth that needed some kind of work. I had a lot of crowns and bridges that were very old and needed to be replaced. By the time I went through all those appointments, I was very convinced to start flossing and doing everything else the dentist told me to do. You see, realizing the result of not doing it gave me a passion to do it. The entire problem was not caused by not flossing, but that did contribute to it.

Tony shared that his brother is a dentist and repeatedly told him that he needed to floss twice daily. He admitted that his mouth and teeth felt better when he did it so he went to a Costco store and bought dozens of little packages of floss. He put them in the bathroom, his car, on his desk at work, where he watched television, and in his gym bag and the laundry room. He put them everywhere so he could not forget to do it. Now he only keeps them in two places because he has formed a habit of flossing. He formed a good habit that will keep him from suffering later on.

Years ago when the western United States was being settled, roads were often just wagon tracks. These rough trails posed serious problems for those who journeyed on them. On one of these winding paths was posted a sign that read, "Avoid this rut or you'll be in it for the next 25 miles." If you don't want to be repeating your bad habit ten years from now, start getting out of the rut now.

I am sure that the person who ends up with lung cancer due to smoking wishes he or she had made the commitment to quit smoking. The person who loses his family due to gambling or alcohol addiction wishes he had been willing to suffer through detox. You see, *if we don't pay the price for freedom, we will end up paying the price for bondage. Either way we will pay a price* because God's law says that we reap what we sow.

Whatever your bad habits may be, take some time and think about what the long-term result of continuing them may be. It might help motivate you to deal with them now.

Let's take one more look at some of the things I am suggesting you do if you want to break a bad habit.

1. Be very committed and willing to suffer for a season if necessary.
2. Be very careful what you say about the habit.
3. Think positive, faith-filled thoughts about your journey.
4. Believe, even when you have not yet seen results.
5. Reflect on what other behaviors your bad habits are connected to and change the pattern.
6. Focus on the one thing you want to change right now.
7. Examine what the dangers of continuing the habit may be.

Happy habit breaking! You're on your way, and I believe you will have success.

CHAPTER
5

Behavior 2: Thoughts, Words, and Habits

What we think leads to the words that come out of our mouths. What we think and speak may be one of our most important habits because it determines the other habits in our lives. In my opinion, thoughts and words are the starting point for forming all good habits and breaking all bad habits.

I am in a beautiful place right now working on this book. I need to go to the gym this morning because I did one of my conferences over the weekend and was unable to work out. I normally work out on Monday, Wednesday, and Friday but could not work out Monday because I was traveling. Today is Tuesday and that means that I really need to do it today. The thought came to me briefly that I could just skip today so I could have more time to write, but since I know the power of thoughts and I also know what I need to do, I didn't entertain the thought. Instead, I said to Dave, "I briefly thought about not working out, but I know that I need to and so I am going to." My thoughts and words could have aided me in doing something I would have regretted later, but instead they helped me keep the habit of exercising regularly.

I had to get rid of the wrong thought as quickly as it came because if I had meditated on it, before long I would have been saying, "I don't really feel like going to the gym today," and shortly after that I would have found an excuse not to go.

This same principle can be applied to any area of your life. When you are trying to develop a good habit or break a bad one, always remember that words precede action. Or, as I frequently say, "Where the mind goes, the man follows."

I have done extensive teaching and writing on the subject of thoughts and words, and I know from experience and God's Word that they are both key factors in success or failure. We must learn to say what we truly want, not what we feel, or even what we currently have. Let's just say that a person sincerely wants to get out of debt, but right now is deeply in debt. That person can think things like, "I am so deeply in debt that I will never get all my bills paid off." Or "This situation I have is impossible to change, it is too late for me."

People who think like this will also talk like this. Their desire may be to be debt free, but their own thoughts and words can prevent them from taking the necessary steps to accomplish what they want to do. They will stay stuck in the rut they are in unless they start agreeing with God's Word that teaches us that all things are possible with God. Such people should start purposely thinking, "It is not God's will for me to be in bondage to debt, and I am going to do all I can to get out of debt. If I do what I can do, God will do what I cannot do. This may take a long time, but I will stick with it until I am free." Thinking like this will give them a mind-set geared toward victory. It will change their words as well as their entire attitude.

We can literally talk ourselves into victory or defeat. We cannot merely get anything we think and say, but we can have anything that God says we can have in His Word. Don't ever settle for anything less than the best that God offers you. This is one of the main reasons we need the Word habit. If we know what God promises in His Word, we can have direction and be encouraged to go for the best that God offers us. God's Word says that we should owe no man anything except to love him (Romans 13:8), so why should we settle for being in debt all our life? We shouldn't and we don't have to.

Jesus told people that they would have what they believed (Matthew 9:29). They had to renew their minds to think like God thinks, so they could have the blessings that God wanted them to have. I hope this is not the first time you have heard this principle, but if it is, please believe that this amazing and powerful truth works for everyone who will work it. God's Word is always the same, and it has the power to change things. But we are not all the same. Some will believe God's Word and do what it says and others will not. Anyone who refuses to believe or is too lazy to make the effort to follow God's instructions will keep their bad habits that are producing bad results in their life. Likewise, anyone who is willing to learn and change can break bad habits and form good ones.

I Can't Help It!

As you learn that you can change the things in your life that are unfruitful and causing you problems, the devil will offer you many excuses to stay the way you are. One of the things you can expect to hear in your head as I share with you the importance of your thoughts and words is, "I can't help what I think. The thoughts just come whether I want them or not." While it is true that thoughts come without being invited, it is not true that you cannot do anything about them. God's Word teaches us to cast down, or refute, wrong thoughts (2 Corinthians 10:5). That simply means we are not to allow them to stay in our mind. You can get rid of any thought you don't want by simply deciding to think something else.

Verbal affirmation helps in this process. If I am thinking, "I don't want to go to the gym today," but know in my heart that I should go, one part of me (my spirit) wants to go while another part (my flesh) doesn't want to. I can say out loud, "I am going to the gym today." What I say interrupts what I am thinking and gives me something new to meditate on.

If you believe the lie that you can't help what you think, then you will never change. Take responsibility for your thoughts and words and begin choosing them carefully because they are the raw material for your actions.

God's Good Plan

God's plan for each of us is good. Who would not want a good plan for their life? I am sure we all do, but we are not all willing to do what it takes to get it. Wanting something is not enough... we must also take action! The apostle Paul teaches us that God has a good plan, a perfect will for each of us, but we must renew our minds according to His Word if we want to prove it out in our experience (Romans 12:2). This Scripture is a key to success. Another Scripture that teaches us the same principal is Joshua 1:8.

> This Book of the Law shall not depart out of your mouth, but you shall meditate on it day and night, that you may observe *and* do according to all that is written in it. For then you shall make your way prosperous, and then you shall deal wisely *and* have good success.

This says it all as far as I am concerned. God's Word must be something we think and talk about regularly and in all situations. If we do—and that *if* must not be ignored—then we will see what we are to do, we will do it, and we will have success. God had given Joshua a tremendous opportunity to lead the Israelites the remainder of the way to the Promised Land that Moses had not conquered. He was told to fear not, be strong and courageous, and keep thinking on and speaking God's Word in order to accomplish the goal in front of him.

What would you like to accomplish in your life? What would you like to change starting right now? Do you have some bad habits that you want to break and some good ones that you want to make? What you want won't happen unless you learn to think and speak in accordance with your desire.

One Good Habit Leads to Another

I believe that forming the habit of thinking and speaking good things will definitely lead to many other good habits. The power of life and death are in the tongue, and they who indulge in it must eat the fruit of it (for death or life) (Proverbs 18:21). If we develop the habit of speaking life at all times, we will have life and have it more abundantly. However, if we speak death (negative things), that will be our experience. The writer of Proverbs stated that we will be filled with the fruit of our mouth and that we must be satisfied with the consequences of the words we choose to speak, whether good or bad (Proverbs 18:20). I have been studying, teaching, and writing on these Scriptures for more than thirty years and they still amaze me. Do we realize the power that God has given us in the choice of our words? I don't think we do, for if we did, surely we would make better choices.

This must be a matter of constant prayer, for no man can tame the tongue without God's help (James 3:8). Hundreds of Scripture verses are about the tongue and the mouth and words. I have most of them underlined in my Bible, and quite often I go through and simply remind myself of the power of my words. I also pray about this area, asking God to let the words of my mouth and the meditation of my heart (thoughts) be acceptable to Him.

Our words can help us or harm us in any area of life. Words are spiritual, for they cannot be seen, and they reach into the spiritual realm and begin to create our future. According to Genesis, God created everything that we see with words! We are created in His image and told to follow His example in all things, so why would our words not work the same way?

Try It!

In 1977, God began showing me the power of my words. I had never heard any teaching like I'm presenting to you in this book, but God convinced me that I was a very negative person who needed major change. He showed me that my words were negative and that my life could not change until my words did. I made a list of things that I wanted to see happen in my life and found Scriptures to back each of them up. Then, for six months, two times a day, I spoke those things out loud. When I started the project, not one of the things I was confessing was a reality in my life, but today they all are. I might add that I still confess those things and other portions of God's precious promises on a regular basis. I suggest you try it. I believe if you consistently think and speak positive, good, life-filled things, you will see changes in yourself and your life that you will like.

I was recently speaking to a woman at an appointment and I said something about speaking positively. She quickly said, "I don't believe in all that positive affirmation junk; I believe in reality!" I felt sad for her because she obviously did not know God's Word and was not aware that she could change her reality by believing, thinking, and speaking in agreement with God. I am so glad that we don't have to settle for reality! Today, reality television shows are very popular, and they are increasing all the time. I would rather have some life-changing power instead of more reality. I want hope and the faith that with God all things are possible.

Make the habit of thinking and speaking according to what you want to see happen in your life part of every other habit you want to develop or destroy. For example, if you are indecisive, don't keep saying, "I have a hard time making decisions." Start saying, "I have God's wisdom (1 Corinthians 1:30) and the mind of Christ (1 Corinthians 2:16) and I am a decisive person." Or if you tend to overeat and need to improve your health and perhaps lose some weight, don't say over and over, "I just can't control my appetite. When I start eating I can't quit until I am stuffed. I have to have sugar every day." If you keep saying what you have, you will always have it. But if you change what you believe by meditating on God's Word and speaking in agreement with it, then you can have what God says you can have. His Word says that He has given us a spirit of discipline and self-control (2 Timothy 1:7), and we should say the same thing.

I am sure that you understand what I am saying, and I pray that you are convinced that you need to start doing it. As I said, try it! Your experience will convince you, even if I can't. You will feel better and have more energy if you speak things that minister life to you, and all the people around you will enjoy you much more.

Please remember that you can't just decide to do this and be successful. No man can tame the tongue. You are going to need a lot of help from God today and every day, and so do I. The mouth is like a wild beast that is unruly and undisciplined (James 3:7–8), but God can change all of that if we will make a commitment and stick with it until we see success.

Reprogram the Computer

What we think and speak, especially if it is frequent, is written on the tablet of our heart. It is embedded in our hard drive, so to speak. Just as a computer can only put out the information that is programmed into it, our hearts can only put out what is written on them. If we don't like the result we are getting from our computer, we don't hesitate to get a new program, and that is what I am suggesting that you do with your life. Start rewriting what has been programmed into your heart. What is on a computer program determines the information that comes out of it, and what is in our heart comes out of our mouth.

For out of the fullness (the overflow, the superabundance) of the heart the mouth speaks.

Matthew 12:34b

I want to assure you that you can do this with God's help. You may have many bad mental and verbal habits, but they can be changed into positive, life-filled ones. It is time to renew your mind and become the person God wants you to be in every area of life.

You Are Filled with Possibilities

The good will of God for us is not going to just happen with no effort on our part, but it is possible if we listen, learn, and are willing to change with His help. Change takes time, but it is time well spent because it brings a great reward. We all spend our time on something, so why not spend it on something that will produce benefits to us and our families and friends? It is possible to change. Truthfully, you are filled with possibilities!

As a child of God, He dwells in you, and all that He is is available to you through faith in Him and His promises. You can know God and have intimate fellowship with Him. You can enjoy a life that will leave a legacy for others. God loves you, and He has created you in a unique and special way. No one can do what you can do, exactly the way you can do it. God wants you to learn to enjoy yourself and every moment of your life, but that cannot happen unless you develop habits that are life-giving instead of life-draining. The habit of right thoughts and words is one of the most important habits to have, and it will open the door to many other good habits that will lead you into the best life possible for you.

CHAPTER
6

Behavior 3: The Habit of Being Decisive

> In any moment of decision the best thing you can
> do is the right thing, the next best thing you can
> do is the wrong thing, and the worst thing you
> can do is nothing.
>
> *Theodore Roosevelt*

People who stay in the middle of the road get run over. Forming the habit of making decisions in a wise and timely manner is vital to our peace and success in life. Thankfully, there are some people who learn to do that. However, some people make decisions too quickly, others make them too slowly, some make them unwisely, and some don't make them at all.

Life is filled with decisions. We all make numerous decisions daily. We decide how late we will sleep, what we will eat, wear, and do with our time. We make employment decisions, relationship decisions, financial decisions, and most importantly we make spiritual decisions. Even people who won't make decisions are still making a decision not to decide. Take a few minutes and honestly evaluate which of the categories mentioned above you fit into. If you are a decisive person and feel that for the most part you make wise decisions, then you are blessed and part of a relatively small group. If you fall into one of the categories of making decisions too quickly, too slowly, or without forethought or wisdom, then this is a great opportunity for you to decide to start forming the habit of being decisive in a proper manner.

If we make right spiritual decisions—and that means we decide to put God first in all things—then the rest of our decisions will be easier. However, making decisions is still something we all labor with at times. For the person who wants to please God in all things, making moral decisions can be easy because God's Word gives us instructions concerning right and wrong behavior. We only need to decide to learn and obey God in what He teaches us to do. But there are many other decisions we must make in daily life that are not specifically covered in God's Word. What do we do about those things? The person who truly wants to please God may fall into the trap of being indecisive due to the fear of displeasing God by doing the wrong thing.

The Misery of Indecision

There is no more miserable human being than one in whom nothing is habitual but indecision.

William James

I can truthfully say that indecision is very unpleasant for me. I am generally a very decisive person and can even be guilty at times of making decisions too quickly. I try not to do that at this stage in my life because I have done it in the past and then regretted the quick decision I made. Unfortunately I still had to deal with the results of it. But even though I fit into the category of being a decisive person, there are still times when I find myself vacillating between two things and having difficulty settling on one or the other. Most of the time it is simply because I don't want to do anything I am not convinced God approves of. I would like to be able to know for certain what God wants me to do in every situation, but I don't, and like everyone else I must step out in faith and eventually do one thing or the other. And, like everyone else, I get butterflies in my tummy and pray with all my heart that if what I am doing is wrong, God will graciously close the door or stop me before I make a huge mistake.

It is impossible to learn how to make good decisions without having the experience of making decisions. We make some right ones and some wrong ones while we are in the process of learning, so I urge you to get started being decisive and learn from your experiences. Whatever you do, don't live your life frozen in fear, always being confused because you don't know what to do.

"Sir, what is the secret of your success?" a reporter asked a bank president.

"Two words."

"And, sir, what are they?"

"Good decisions."

"And how do you make good decisions?"

"One word."

"And, sir, what is that?"

"Experience."

"And how do you get experience?"

"Two words."

"And, sir, what are they?"

"Bad decisions."

—*Anonymous*

The apostle James, being directed by the Holy Spirit, teaches that if we need wisdom we are to ask for it, and God will give it. Only it must be in faith that we ask with no wavering (no hesitating, no doubting). If we do waver, hesitate, or doubt, we become unstable and unreliable in all of our ways and we are unable to receive from the Lord anything we ask for (James 1:5–8). These Scriptures make the position of the indecisive person quite clear. He is going to be miserable, confused, and unable to get help from God. We must approach God in faith, ready to take action when we have assurance in our heart of some direction. If after prayer and waiting we still feel that we have no direction, then it may mean that God is simply giving us the freedom to make our own choice.

More than once in my life as I have been seeking God concerning what to do in a situation, He has whispered in my heart, "You can do what you want to do." I have learned in those situations that God places desires in my heart and that I am free to follow them. That kind of freedom frightens some people, but if we know God's Word, then we should know His heart and we can live accordingly. Dave and I have four grown children. When they were young we told them everything to do and not to do, but as they grew we gradually released more and more decision-making power to them, trusting that they had learned what we would want them to do and that they would follow that. They didn't always make the right decisions, but through trial and error they learned to make decisions and be responsible for their outcomes, which is part of being an adult.

We grow as children of God just as our natural children grow, and He doesn't always give us exact and specific directions. He expects us to follow His Word, His Spirit, and His Wisdom. If we don't have peace about something, or it would not be wise to do it, then we should not do it. It is just that simple! One thing is for sure, and that is that we don't have to be afraid to make decisions. If we do make a decision that turns out to be wrong, then we can modify it as we go along. God will help us get where we are going, but He can't drive a parked car. If you sincerely want God's will and you get lost as you travel through life, God will find you and get you back on the right path.

"Do something, lest you do nothing" is a favorite saying of mine. Some people waste their entire life doing nothing because they won't make a decision. The reasons for being indecisive can be varied, so let's look at some of them:

1. A person may be indecisive because their parents never allowed them to make their own decisions. The parents may have thought they were protecting their children, but they actually crippled their ability to be decisive.

2. Indecisive people may be insecure about themselves and their abilities. This is the case with a great many people in our

society. Satan loves to give us many fears and insecurities that immobilize us and prevent us from fulfilling our destiny. Indecisive people must learn how much and how perfectly God loves them and that they can do all things through Christ Who gives them strength, ability, and wisdom.

3. Being a people pleaser can also make a person indecisive. People pleasers always look for the approval of others and never follow their own heart when making decisions. It is rather sad how much we depend on the approval and acceptance of other people. If we live our life to please other people, we will end up never living our life at all. We will merely let others live their lives through us when we do what they want instead of what we want.

4. Some people are simply afraid to be wrong. They may be too proud to be able to deal with the thought of having made a wrong decision, so they make no decision at all. They are always trying to decide and never doing it. I often say that the only way we can find out if we are right is to step out and find out. Being right all the time is highly overrated. Being wrong only hurts our pride for a few moments, but being indecisive hurts us in ways that are almost too great to calculate.

5. Once a decision is made, action must follow. Some people may stay indecisive simply to keep themselves from having to be responsible for the work that always follows a decision. Successful men and women are wise in making decisions and persistent and determined in the action they must take thereafter.

In all of these reasons I am offering for indecision, one thing is for sure: It is a bad habit and can be eliminated by forming good habits. Make a courageous decision to be decisive. The more practice you get, the better you will get at doing it.

How to Make Decisions

Perhaps some practical advice on how to make decisions will help you get started.

Make a list of your options. How many different ways can you go? If you want to change jobs, for example, what would your options be? Do you want to change careers or get another job within the field you are experienced in? You may simply want to decide what to do today. You have the day free, so what are your options? You can finish a project that you started and did not complete, or you can go shopping and to lunch with a friend, or you can visit your elderly parents you have not seen in way too long, or you could lie on the couch and watch television all day. What is the best thing to do?

Truthfully, you are the only one who can decide. You might have more fun shopping and eating, but you might have more long-term peace if you finish your project. And, if you're wise with your time, you can probably work in the visit to your parents with either one of the other options. Lying on the couch all day probably isn't a good option because you will end up tired and feeling as if you wasted your day.

If you want to buy something, you can buy it and have the thing, or not buy it and have your money. Which of the two options will best suit you in the long run? Asking ourselves some questions about options is often a huge help in making decisions. After all, how can we make really good decisions if we don't even know what our choices are?

Weigh the possible outcome. For every option there is a possible outcome, and we can label it positive or negative. Dave and I are in the process of making a decision right now, and just this morning I told him I have a list of the positives and the negatives, and the positives do outweigh the negatives. Realizing that helped us make our decision.

It is always unwise to make decisions without taking time to consider what the possible outcome of that decision may be. If you are trying to decide whether to make a commitment of your time and energy to anything, especially if it is something that is a long-term commitment, think everything through completely.

How much of your time will this take? Do you honestly have the time to give to it without overloading your schedule? If you are going to commit, do you need to eliminate something else from your schedule first? How will this commitment affect your family? Are you saying yes to something that someone else wants you to do, but honestly you would rather not do it? If you make the commitment will you find yourself complaining about having to do it? Always think about the outcome of every decision, or you will regret many of the decisions that you make.

Acknowledge God. The writer of Proverbs, the book of wisdom, teaches us to acknowledge God in **all** of our ways. We should ask God to lead us at the start of trying to make any decision, but we should also look to Him once we feel we do know what we should do, just to make sure He is in agreement. Do you have peace? Is it wise? Are your motives for doing it right? Wait on God for a little while to give Him an opportunity to let you know if there is anything that you are not considering.

We should never make our plans and then pray for God to bless them. We should pray before any planning takes place. If the true desire of your heart is to follow God in all things, He will let you know one way or another if you are doing the right thing.

Start Small

You may be thinking, "Joyce, what if I have done all of these things and I still don't know what decision to make?" If that is the case, my advice is to take a baby step in faith and see if what you are committing to is going to be right for you. This isn't possible in every decision, but it is in many.

For example, if someone is asking you to join a committee, you could commit for a month and then see how you feel about it before you commit for a year or more. Don't ever hesitate to be honest with people, letting them know that making the right decision is very important to you and that you don't want to make a long-term commitment without testing the water, so to speak. I always stick my toe in swimming pool water before jumping in, simply because I don't want to be shocked by its temperature. If the first step works, then take another and another.

All great things began as small things. People with great faith began by exercising their small faith, and as they did they experienced the faithfulness of God and their faith grew. Our ministry began as a Bible study in our home. The first five years we had twenty-five people in attendance. Now we have a worldwide ministry with offices in eighteen countries.

God's Word encourages us not to despise the days of small beginnings, so if you are an indecisive person I suggest that you start being decisive in small areas first. Make quicker decisions about what you want to eat, wear, or do with your time today. I have been out to eat with people who can look at a menu for forty-five minutes before deciding what they want. Even when they order they might say, "I still don't know what I want, so I guess I will just order this." I can understand taking a little time to decide, but being in that much indecision is probably an indicator of a deeper problem.

We all know what happens to our day if we begin with the attitude of getting out of bed and waiting to see what happens. I had a friend once who called me each morning to see what I was going to do that day. We spent a lot of time together and she didn't want to make any plans until she knew what I was doing. I would often respond by asking, "What are you going to do today?" She would say, "I don't know, I thought I would see what you are doing." This kind of extreme passivity and vagueness is dangerous. Don't ever let someone else's decisions be the guide for yours.

I like to say, "Have a plan and be ready to change it if God interrupts you for something He needs." It is possible to plan too much, but to have no plan at all is the seed for a wasted life.

Once you do make a decision, even a small one, try to stick to it. God is not the author of confusion; therefore, don't become confused through excessive reasoning about your choice. I love the Scripture that says, "Set your minds and keep them set" (Colossians 3:2). Sadly, we are often too easily distracted and have difficulty keeping our mind set in a direction. Develop the habit of being decisive; don't be double-minded, don't vacillate, hesitate, waver, or doubt. Start confessing daily that you are a decisive person and that you make wise decisions.

CHAPTER
7

Behavior 4: Healthy Habits

The more good habits you develop, the less you will have to fight with bad ones. I am a strong believer in concentrating on good things rather than bad ones. Healthy habits actually solve a lot of other bad habits. For example, if I feel healthy and energetic I am more likely to be easy to get along with, and I don't have to deal with the bad habit of being grouchy. When I feel good, I am happier, friendlier, and I display more patience.

The world is filled with unhealthy people. Billions of dollars are spent on visits to doctors and on medicines and treatments to help us feel better. Probably millions of hours are spent on our illnesses, when many of them could have been avoided by making healthy habits earlier in life.

Please don't wait until you are sick to choose health. An ounce of prevention is worth a pound of cure. In my book *Look Great, Feel Great* I cover many principles of prevention in detail, but in this chapter I want to speak to you about some of the ones that are perhaps the most urgent for all of us.

Your Body Is God's House

> You were bought with a price [purchased with a precious-
> ness and paid for, made His own]. So then, honor God *and*
> bring glory to Him in your body.
>
> *1 Corinthians 6:20*

Are you an investor or a gambler? Are you investing in good health now so you'll reap benefits later? Or are you gambling that you can do nothing, or even abuse yourself by having many unhealthy bad habits, and get by with it? Sadly, many people are gamblers where their health is concerned, but they are not wise. A wise man will invest in his own self by making choices that will keep him healthy and strong not only in the present but in later years as well. Just as a wise financial investor will do without some things now in order to invest for the future, so we should discipline ourselves to conserve our energy and health.

According to God's Word, we are His temple, or His house. He lives in us. The Old Testament instructions on how to build, decorate, and care for the temple were detailed and abundant. It was not supposed to fall into disrepair due to periods of negligence, and if it did, entire programs were designed to rebuild and repair it. Do you need a fresh coat of paint, or do you need an entire program to rebuild and repair your health? If you need to develop healthy habits, put them at the top of your list of habits to develop, possibly right after developing the habit of spending time with God. Because your health affects you and all the people you are in relationship with in a variety of ways. One of the ways we can show our love and appreciation for God is by being good stewards of the health He gives us. Your body is the vehicle you need to get around the earth in, and if you destroy it you cannot go to a store and purchase another one. God has a destiny for you, and there is some special assignment that only you can fulfill. It is important that you live long enough to do whatever it is that God has assigned to you.

Late in 2006, I got tired of feeling tired too much of the time and not liking the way I was starting to look physically. So I went on a program to rebuild and repair my body. I felt that God had shown me that if I didn't begin to exercise regularly, I would not be strong for the last third of my journey here on earth. It is very important to me that I finish what God has me here for, so I took His instruction seriously.

I signed a one-year contract at a gym, secured a trainer and nutritionist, and went to work. Years later I am very glad I took action when I did. Yes, I was sore much of the time and I missed some of the fatty, sweet foods I was accustomed to eating, but I survived, and before long I had developed healthier habits. It required, and still requires, an investment of my time, but I believe I am a better person today than I was then in many ways.

Mark Twain said, "The only way to keep your health is to eat what you don't want, drink what you don't like and do what you'd rather not." In many ways this is a true statement, but the good news is that even though you may start out not liking some of the things you will need to do, eventually you will become accustomed to them and you will crave them as much as you now dislike them. If I have to miss going to the gym for a few days, my muscles actually crave the workout. Sounds impossible, I know, but it is true.

Today I am craving vegetables and will have several different grilled or steamed vegetables for lunch. I can hardly believe it myself, but I am being truthful. Our bodies are not really all that intelligent. They just crave what we repeatedly give them. If it is bad, they will want what is bad, and if it is good, they will want that. You can retrain yourself to enjoy healthy choices in all areas of life.

There are many wonderful books available on nutrition that will help you if you are uneducated in this area. Do yourself a favor and purchase and read one of them, because the knowledge you gain will renew your mind and help you make healthier choices. Of course I recommend my own book *Look Great, Feel Great*, and I also recommend Dr. Don Colbert's books. He is a wonderful Christian doctor and nutritionist, and he has helped thousands of people develop healthy habits. We perish for a lack of knowledge, so be willing to educate yourself in any area where you need help.

De-Stress

Stress is the disease of the twenty-first century. It is the culprit behind a large percentage (I have heard numbers as high as 80 percent) of our illnesses. Our bodies are built to handle stress unless it becomes excessive and repetitive. When it does, we are in danger of many unhealthy results. If you want to improve your health, you must make a decision to not allow excessive stress in your life. Life probably won't change, so that means you will have to change how you approach and respond to life. For example, worry, anxiety, and fear are major stressors, and we can eliminate them by trusting God and casting our care on Him.

Excessive stress produces too much of the hormone cortisol in our body, and this is dangerous. People can actually become addicted to it, like a drug. The more they live with the gas pedal of their life pressed to the floor, the more stressed out they feel, and they hate it, but they become so accustomed to it that they crave it. They don't know how to rest and relax. People brag about living in the fast lane of life, but truthfully that is where all the wrecks take place. Most people, when asked if they were too busy, would say yes. But interestingly enough, they are the only ones who can make the decision to change lanes. Most people complain all the time about their schedules, but they never do anything about them. To complain and do nothing to make one's situation better is a total waste of time and very foolish.

Here is what even a little cortisol does in your body. It sends your heart into overdrive, pounding at four times its natural rate, and it does the same thing for your lungs. It constricts your blood vessels and raises your blood pressure to dangerous levels.

It dries up your mouth and shuts down your stomach and intestines. It drains the blood from your face and skin. It scrambles your immune system. It wrecks your sleep, turns off sexual interest and reproductive capability, slows healing, and increases your risk of periodontal disease, skin disease, and autoimmune diseases. It turns off short-term memory and rational thought. It actually shrinks part of your brain. It even makes you overeat. We know that many people overeat due to stress. It is one of those patterns we talked about earlier. When they feel stressed, they habitually go to food to find comfort.

Sounds like bad news, doesn't it? You'd think that people would go out of their way to steer clear of this "drug." Yet we give ourselves doses of it every day. I was addicted to it for many years of my life. As I said, we can handle normal amounts of stress. Cortisol is helpful when you need to respond to a stressful incident, like avoiding hitting a car when someone suddenly pulls in front of you on the highway. All of the physical effects of cortisol take place in the body, but the body soon returns to normal when the danger has passed and the stress is over. But when stress is continual, it wears your body out. It is impossible to be healthy and maintain high levels of stress over a long period of time. Develop the habit of living wisely now so you won't be worn-out by the time you are forty or fifty years old.

If you have already spent years not taking care of yourself and you are sick, tired, and worn-out, don't think it is too late for you. Start developing healthy habits right now, and every good choice you make now will begin repairing any damage that has been done. It is never too late to begin.

Start paying attention to what causes you to experience stress and make changes. It is as simple as that, and if you make it more complicated, you will more than likely never change. No matter how many reasons and excuses we have for living with stress, the truth is that we can eliminate a lot of stress from our lives if we truly want to.

Seven Pillars for Good Health

Dr. Don Colbert recommends the following seven pillars for good health. These are all simple, basic things, but they can also be life-changing if we make them healthy habits in our life.

1. Drink lots of water

The experts say we should drink half of our body weight in water every day. I know you might think, "If I did that I would drown." But drinking plenty of water will improve your metabolism and can help you lose weight. It also increases your energy level. The more water you drink, the more you will want to drink. If you're not drinking enough water, start immediately. Drink pure, clean water, and if you can't get it from your home faucet, then purchase a filter for it or buy bottled water. The best way to form the habit of drinking water is to keep it with you at all times. Keep water as your main drink at home. The fewer choices you have in your refrigerator or cabinets, the more inclined you will be to choose water.

Many people say they don't like water, but it is only because they are not accustomed to drinking it. Remember, your body will eventually crave what you give it. My father did not like water and wouldn't drink it, and he died with kidney failure. Water is the only thing that properly cleanses our bodies of dangerous toxins. Most of our body is made up of water, and as water evaporates all the time, we must continually replace it.

2. Get plenty of sleep and rest

I can already hear the excuses bombarding your brain. You don't have enough time to sleep the recommended eight hours a night. But the truth is that if you don't do so, you are probably running out of time faster than you think. Some people don't need as much sleep as others, but most of us need all we can get. If you are tired a lot, one of the first things to ask yourself is, "Am I getting enough sleep?" Our lives can be shortened by not getting sleep and rest. The mind doesn't function properly without it, and our immune systems are compromised and more apt to become unable to fight off disease.

It is very interesting to me that God created us with the ability to shut everything off and sleep. Our bodies go into a state of renewal and repair during our sleep, and we are refreshed mentally, emotionally, and physically for the next day. A lot of people have trouble sleeping and perhaps need medical attention, but more often than not the inability to sleep is stress related.

Learning how to rest will also help you sleep better. I need about three to four hours in the evening to rest. When I get it, I sleep very well 99.9 percent of the time. I have developed a habit of going to sleep by 9 p.m. and getting up at 5 a.m. unless I am traveling and teaching, and that works well for me with the rest of my lifestyle. I believe it is one of the reasons why I feel as good as I do and can accomplish as much as I do even though I will be seventy years young on my next birthday. My schedule may not work for you, and I am not suggesting it needs to, but you should have a regular bedtime and try to get seven to eight hours of sleep a night.

Rest is commanded in the Word of God. God instituted the Sabbath not only for worship but also for rest. We need to honor the Sabbath principle in our lives by resting regularly. Most of the people I talk to are tired, and they talk about their need to get some rest, or some time off, or some time to themselves. But talk alone doesn't help us improve our health. We must take action. Develop the healthy habit of regular sleep and rest and you will enjoy the rest of your life much more.

3. Eat quality food

Dr. Colbert calls quality food *living food*, and it is vital if we want to get the nutrients we need for our body. Eating the things that grow naturally on the earth, such as plenty of fruits and vegetables, is one of the best places to start your journey toward healthy habits. These living foods are high in nutrition and fiber. Buy quality food (organic if possible) that will taste good to you and you will enjoy it much more. Sadly, most prepackaged foods have had the natural nutrients stripped out of them and unhealthy preservatives have been added for longer shelf life.

Learn to read labels and you will be amazed at what you might be dumping into your body. If you're making food choices for your family as well as for yourself, the importance of doing so is multiplied.

Eat more fish, chicken, and turkey and less fatty red meat. If at all possible, eat organic meat or meat that is hormone free. The saying that we are what we eat is more truthful than we may want to admit.

I am sure you are wondering if you can eat any dessert, and my answer would be yes, in moderation. Some nutritionists and health experts will tell you to eat no sugar, but I already know that is not very likely to happen unless you are one of those unusual people who simply don't like sweets. I eat dessert two times a week, and that works for me. I enjoy it when I have it, and I don't feel deprived, but it is not excessive. I eat healthily and exercise, so I feel my body can handle a little sugar twice a week. Dave is sensitive to sugar and almost never eats it. We are all different, so you will have to develop your own eating plan with God's help, and I believe that He will guide you based on your body's unique needs.

One of the cardinal guidelines about healthy eating is to do all things in moderation while having as much variety in your diet as possible. Also, please enjoy your food. I believe God gave us taste buds for a reason and He intends for us to enjoy the food we eat.

Solving the Weight Issue

I know that many people struggle with being overweight and that losing weight can become the focus of their lives. I too was overweight for many years and lived on various diets, none of which worked long-term. I finally realized that the answer was that I needed a healthy lifestyle, not another diet. I believe that if you will focus on being healthy instead of on being skinny, you will eventually reach the weight that is right for you.

4. Exercise

The value of exercise is tremendous. After I had been working out at the gym for one year, my coach told me that even if I quit right then, I would still benefit for fifteen years from the one year I had put into it. There are multiple forms of exercise, and I simply want to urge you to select one that suits you, one you can learn to enjoy and turn into a habit. Walk, ride a bicycle, swim, play an active sport, exercise with weights, or get an exercise video. The choices are endless, so choose one and get started. Even if you feel that you cannot do a lot, doing something is better than doing nothing.

5. Supplements

Not everyone wants to take vitamins and other supplements, and that choice will need to be yours. Dave and I both take plenty of supplements because we want to do all we can to make sure we are nutritionally sound. My advice would be to take at least a multivitamin daily, some extra vitamin D, and anything else you might specifically be in need of. For example, some people need to take iron but others don't. If you want to take supplements but you tend to forget, then do something to help you remember. Put them where you will have to see them, or write a note to yourself, or set the alarm on your phone.

6. Detox

We all have toxic buildup in our bodies, and those toxins need to be eliminated. Toxic buildup can be the root cause of a lot of physical ailments. Some toxins are expelled through breathing, and many others are expelled through the kidneys and bowels. Exercise makes us sweat, and that is another excellent way to detoxify. Home saunas as well as other methods of detoxification are available that you may want to look into.

7. Coping with stress

We have already discussed stress in this chapter, and it is included on Dr. Colbert's list. I want to reemphasize the vital importance of eliminating as much stress from your life as is possible.

You may need to develop several healthy habits to feel that you have attained optimum health, and if that is the case, don't feel overwhelmed. You might start by locating something that you eat too much of and either cut it out completely or learn to eat it in moderation. Perhaps you could begin to rest and relax one hour a day and see what a difference it makes. Try using some of your lunch hour at work to take a walk. Just make some decisions, get started, and be determined to enjoy a healthy, vibrant, and energetic life.

CHAPTER
8

Behavior 5: The Happy Habit

Happy is the man who finds wisdom, and the man who gains understanding.

Proverbs 3:13 NKJV

Everyone in the world wants to be happy. As a matter of fact, I believe that desire is the main thing that motivates us in most of what we do. But do we truly know what makes us genuinely happy? And is happiness just a feeling or an emotion that we search for, or is it deeper than that?

Abraham Lincoln said, "People are as happy as they make up their mind to be." I agree. I am convinced that happiness is a choice and a habit that we can develop. First we choose happiness, and then feelings will follow. The psalmist David said, "This is the day which the Lord has brought about; we will rejoice and be glad in it" (Psalm 118:24). The statement "we will" is the deciding factor in the enjoyment of our day. If you don't decide to be happy, there will always be something to steal your joy and poison your happiness.

Jesus told us that in the world we will have tribulation, and His suggestion was to cheer up (John 16:33). Joy gives us strength to handle the problems we do have. Sadness of any kind drains our energy and breaks our spirit. One of the best habits you can develop is the happy habit. The more happy days you experience, the more you will refuse to be unhappy. Being unhappy about anything is a waste of time and changes nothing, so why do it?

> Each morning when I open my eyes I say to myself: I, not events, have the power to make me happy or unhappy today. I can choose which it shall be. Yesterday is dead, tomorrow hasn't arrived yet. I have just one day, today, and I'm going to be happy in it.
>
> *Groucho Marx*

It sounds like Groucho Marx agreed with the psalmist David, who agreed with God. God wants us to be happy and to enjoy life. Jesus said that He came so that we might have and enjoy our lives abundantly (John 10:10). Will you make a decision to make Jesus happy by being happy yourself?

Another similar thought that is powerful is "Yesterday is history, tomorrow is a mystery, and today is a present."

Focus

When we focus our time and attention on things we find to be bad, we feel sad, angry, or anxious. Focusing on good things makes us feel good, excited, energized, and enthusiastic. It has been said that focusing on good things is the first law of happiness because what we focus on (think about) determines our feelings. God has given us the ability to choose happiness no matter what is going on around us. I am not suggesting that we ignore our problems, but there is a big difference between focusing on them and working to solve or resolve them.

You will never be consistently happy if you believe that happiness is determined by what is happening around you or to you. Do you believe that you can choose happiness and make it a habit? If you do, then it is time to get to work on repositioning yourself and your perspective by putting the best possible construction on everything. A negative person cannot be happy, and a persistently positive person cannot be unhappy, at least not for long.

Examine Your Goals

Are you reaching for the right thing? We often think that something will make us happy if we can attain it, only to be disappointed when we reach our goal and discover we are still as unhappy as we were before. Experience teaches us that things can't keep us happy for very long. Multitudes of people have had the experience of putting their careers ahead of everything. They work an excessive number of hours, ignoring the development of personal and family relationships, and often end up wealthy and lonely and possibly sick. They can buy anything they want but have no one to share it with, and even if they did, they wouldn't feel good enough to enjoy it.

Good relationships and good health are two of the things that feed happiness, and they should be at the top of our list of goals.

As I have already said, our number one goal should be to develop a close, intimate, personal relationship with God through Jesus Christ. Being in continual fellowship with God and learning to obey Him in all things will make you happier than you might ever imagine. Since God is Life, how can we hope to enjoy life apart from Him? If people are so busy trying to climb the ladder of success that they have no time for God, they may reach the top, but they will find that their ladder has been leaning against the wrong building. They have spent their lives trying to get somewhere but find that it isn't where they want to be after all.

In my personal search for happiness, I discovered that my joy is fed by doing things for other people. If we live to make others happy, God will bring a harvest of joy into our lives. Loving God and people is the key to daily happiness for me. No matter what kind of problem I have, if I focus on what I can do to put a smile on another person's face, I find that it makes me happy. Psychologist Greta Palmer said, "Those only are happy who have their minds on some object other than their own happiness... On the happiness of others...On the improvement of mankind."

Regarding serving others, Jesus said, "If you know these things, blessed and happy and to be envied are you if you practice them (if you act accordingly and really do them)" (John 13:17).

What Do You Believe?

Our personal beliefs can greatly affect our level of joy and happiness. We need to believe that God loves us and that we have a purpose in life. Purposeless people are frequently very unhappy as well as people who feel unloved. You are loved and God has His eye on you at all times. He has a good plan for your life and He needs you to fulfill your role in His master plan.

Do you believe that there is hope for change no matter what your current circumstances are? I have found that hopeful people are some of the happiest people in the world. Hope is powerful. Consider the following Scriptures:

> Moreover [let us also be full of joy now!] let us exult *and* triumph in our troubles *and* rejoice in our sufferings, knowing that pressure *and* affliction *and* hardship produce patient *and* unswerving endurance.
>
> And endurance (fortitude) develops maturity of character (approved faith and tried integrity). And character [of this sort] produces [the habit of] joyful and confident hope of eternal salvation.
>
> Such hope never disappoints or deludes or shames us ...
>
> *Romans 5:3–5a*

If we will believe that our troubles are working strong character and tried integrity in us, then we can have confident hope and joy even in the midst of them. People who can remain happy no matter what their circumstances are powerful indeed.

Examine your belief system and see if some of your own beliefs are contributing to a lack of happiness in your life. Are you trusting (believing) God in all areas of life? The Bible says in Romans 15:13 that joy and peace are found in believing.

What do you believe about yourself? If you believe you are a failure, unloved, worthless, and that it is too late for you to have a good life, then you must change what you believe about you. Believe what God says about you in His Word, not what others have told you, or even how you merely feel. Change your mind and begin to believe things that will increase your joy.

What Are You Waiting For?

Are you putting off happiness until some other time? I am personally trying to avoid saying, "I will be happy when—" and just being happy now. We fall into the trap of thinking, "I will be happy when it's Friday and I get my paycheck and have the weekend free." Or "I will be happy when vacation time is here," or "when I retire and don't have to work anymore," or "when the kids are grown and my life is my own." There can be a million *whens* that keep us from enjoying *now*. Make a decision not to base your happiness on some future event, and be happy today! It would be better to say, "I will enjoy vacation time when it comes, but I am happy right now."

Learn to enjoy everyday ordinary life because that is what most of life is. We can't base our happiness on the few special events that we have in the course of our life, because if we do, we will miss a lot of happiness. You don't have to be happy just on Friday; you can also be happy on Saturday, Sunday, Monday, Tuesday, Wednesday, and Thursday. Go ahead and try it and you will find out that you can do it if you want to.

The only way we can avoid having regrets tomorrow is to make better choices about today. What will you do with today? It is yours as a gift from God, and I urge you not to waste it being sad over something that your sadness won't change anyway.

Are you waiting for some outside force to move you to feel happy? If so, you may be waiting a long, long time. Form the habit of deciding how you will live each day, without waiting to see how you feel. The only thing to do with life is to enjoy it, and that won't happen unless you form a habit of doing so. If you tend be sad and unhappy (which is also a habit), put some smiley faces around your house to remind you to begin your happiness journey by smiling more. If you smile, it will make you feel a tiny bit happier and you might get addicted to the feeling and want more and more.

Are you waiting for some other person in your life to change his or her behavior so you can be happy? If so, that is a huge mistake. Why should you let someone else's choices determine your level of joy? Besides, nobody else can make you permanently happy—not your spouse, not your child, not your friend.

Melanie is a sixty-year-old woman who has been married for more than forty years. Her husband, Don, is a history professor at a small Christian college. Don has always loved history and he gets tremendous satisfaction from teaching. The Civil War is his passion, and in his free time he writes books about specific battles or key individuals of the war.

One day Melanie confided in a friend that she had been unhappy for years because Don didn't make enough money to provide nice vacations or things that she wanted, like beautiful furnishings for the house or a great wardrobe. Most of the time when Melanie complained her friends would commiserate with her and tell her that she deserved nice things. But this particular friend said, "Melanie, Don is not responsible for your happiness. You are. Don loves his work, he isn't interested in becoming rich, and even if he was, he's sixty years old, so you do the math.

"If you want to be happy, you'd better figure out what you can do about it, because that isn't Don's job."

It is six years later, and Melanie's friend told me that Melanie recently wrote her a letter thanking her for showing tough love. Melanie took responsibility for her own happiness, and she said that her marriage has never been better. Not only that, but she learned that she is a playwright. She has written a play that is performed in regional theaters. She is now happy and fulfilled.

We cannot control people, and the sooner we learn that, the happier we can be. I have realized in the last couple of years that most of my "unhappy days" are caused by things other people do or don't do. Someone might offend me or hurt my feelings. They might be making choices that are hurting them, and because I love them, their choices hurt me. Sometimes people are rude and disrespectful and that hurts me. We do get hurt and disappointed by people, but we don't have to dwell on what they do. We can realize that they are hurting themselves more than they are hurting us and let that knowledge motivate us to pray sincerely for them rather than merely feeling sorry for ourselves and losing our joy.

Take responsibility for your own joy and happiness and never again base it on what someone else does.

Think Less and Laugh More

Laughter is an instant vacation.

Milton Berle

When we laugh we momentarily forget all of our concerns and struggles. Laughter is wonderful! It energizes us and is one of the healthiest things we can do. Sometimes we think too much, trying to figure too many things out, and we become so intense that we forget to laugh at ourselves as well as at many other things in life.

Laughter can pull a person out of depression and despair, and it can turn an ordinary day into a memorable one. My daughter Laura and I seem to be able to laugh at almost anything. We are very different from each other in personality, but our chemistry together is hilarious. Instead of being irritated by our differences, she thinks I am hilarious and I feel that way about her. When we love people unconditionally, we can let them be themselves without being irritated by everything they do that is not the way we would do it.

I strongly urge you to find some people who make you laugh and spend more time with them. Laughter is possibly more important than you know. Dave and I try to laugh as much as we can.

God once told me that I did too much thinking. I was a pretty deep and intense person who wanted to understand all of my actions as well as every person and event in my life. My reasoning only left me confused. I wasted a lot of time trying to understand things that God wasn't ready to explain yet. I had to get comfortable not knowing. Are you able to do that? Can you not know the answer to something and go ahead and enjoy your day, or are you like I was, deep and intense and joyless? I am grateful that God has helped me form the happy habit, and I pray you will begin right away developing yours if you have not already done so.

The average child laughs 150 times a day, while the average adult only laughs four to eight times a day. It is no wonder that God tells us in His Word that we must become like little children. Mark Twain said that our most effective weapon is laughter. You may be thinking, "Well, Joyce, you just don't know how unhappy my life is, and if you did, you wouldn't be telling me to laugh." I realize there are tragic things that happen in life and certainly times when laughter would not be appropriate, but there are many things that we let make us sad when it would be better if we laughed more.

Are You Letting "You" Make You Unhappy?

A root cause of a lot of our unhappiness is simply that we are not happy with ourselves. We are not happy with the way we look, our talents, or our level of perfection. We may compare ourselves with others instead of happily being the person that we are intended to be.

We all make mistakes, and although we want to be serious about the changes that need to be made in our lives, it is also good to learn to laugh at ourselves and not be so intense about every little mistake we make. We all have faults and are likely to have some as long as we are alive, so lighten up and don't take yourself so seriously. Ethel Barrymore said, "You grow up the day you have the first real laugh at yourself." Learn to enjoy yourself!

You are with yourself more than you are with anyone else, so if you can learn to enjoy your own company, it will greatly improve the quality of your life. Don't take a daily inventory of all your faults and lament over them. Trust God to show you what needs to be changed, and work with the Holy Spirit toward those changes. I have changed a lot over the course of thirty-five years of walking with God and still have more changes to go through. I wish I had known how to enjoy myself sooner than I did while I was making the journey, but at least I can give you good advice. Being unhappy with myself didn't make me change any faster, and it won't help you either. I highly encourage you to enjoy every step of your journey toward spiritual maturity.

You Only Live Once

Ready or not, someday your life will come to an end. You don't get a second chance, so be sure you live this one life that you have to the fullest. Your life is a precious gift from God, and it would be tragic if you lived it unhappy. Put the happy habit on your list of good habits to make, and as you develop it, the sad, mad habit will find no place in your life.

Having a life worth living doesn't happen by accident; it's something we must choose to do on purpose. I can truly say that I am a genuinely happy person, but I wasn't that way until I made the choice to be happy.

CHAPTER
9

Behavior 6: The Habit of Faith

All I have seen teaches me to trust the Creator for
all I have not seen.

Ralph Waldo Emerson

Living by faith in God takes the pressure off of us and allows
us to enjoy all of life in a greater way. Faith is God's will, and
I believe it can and should become our habit. The Bible says in
Hebrews 11:6 that without faith we cannot please God. Romans
14:23b says that anything we do that is not done in faith is sin.
Romans 1:17 says that righteousness is revealed in God's Word,
and that it leads us from faith to faith. To me this means that
we should be in faith at all times. It should be our habit! Faith
is trusting in what God says in His Word, even though you may
not have any evidence of its reality yet. Faith is what connects
us to an omnipotent God. When we fail to depend on God's

dependability, we short-circuit faith, bringing two tragic results: powerlessness and hopelessness.

> Now faith is the assurance (the confirmation, the title deed) of the things [we] hope for, being the proof of things [we] do not see *and* the conviction of their reality [faith perceiving as real fact what is not revealed to the senses].
>
> *Hebrews 11:1*

> For we have heard of your faith in Christ Jesus [the leaning of your entire human personality on Him in absolute trust and confidence in His power, wisdom, and goodness] and of the love which you [have and show] for all the saints (God's consecrated ones).
>
> *Colossians 1:4*

These two Scriptures give us a very clear definition of what faith is. Faith fills us with hopeful expectation.

> True faith is never found alone; it is always accompanied by expectation. The man who believes the promises of God expects to see them fulfilled. Where there is no expectation, there is no faith.
>
> *A. W. Tozer*

God's will is for us to live by faith at all times. You might be thinking of all the bad habits that you need to break and all the good ones you need to make, and you feel overwhelmed. Your mind wants to think, "This is just too much, I will never be able to do this." This is where faith comes in. You can say, "I don't know how I am going to do it, but I am expecting God's help. With God all things are possible."

Just make a beginning and keep going day after day. Be encouraged by any progress you make and refuse to be discouraged by how far you think you have to go. God is pleased that you have made a beginning toward forming better habits.

You Have All the Faith You Need

I sometimes hear people say, "I just don't have enough faith for that." But the truth is that we all have all the faith we need to do whatever God's will is for us. "God has dealt to each one a measure of faith" (Romans 12:3 NKJV). We all have faith, but the key to success is where we place it. If you put your faith in you or in other people, you will be disappointed, but if you put it in God, you will be amazed at what He can do through you.

When I sit down at the computer to start writing a new book, even though I have a subject in mind and have done some research, I still don't know for sure what I am going to say. Beginning is sometimes the most difficult. I sit there, look at the keys, then finally put my fingers on the keys and words begin to come to my heart. Then day after day and chapter after chapter, by faith I finally finish the book. I sigh in relief and satisfaction that another project is completed.

Faith requires that we step out. We must *begin*, and if what we are doing is God's will, He will never fail to help us finish if we keep on in faith day after day.

You have faith, but it may need to grow, and that happens as you use it. Little faith can become great faith as you step out on the promises of God. Peter was the only disciple who walked on water, but then he was only one who trusted God enough to get out of the boat. Are you ready to stop merely having an idea of faith and begin taking steps of faith? I think we all begin with the same amount of faith, but some people never use theirs so it never grows. As we take steps of faith to be obedient to God, we experience His faithfulness and our faith becomes strong.

Consider this story of a tightrope walker.

What is faith? One daredevil who was billed as the Great Blonden startled crowds with his death-defying stunts over Niagara Falls. Pointing to the tightrope suspended over one area of Niagara Falls, this brave fellow would taunt the crowds that had gathered by saying, "Who believes that I can push this cart over the falls on the rope?" Hands shot up all over the crowds. The Great Blonden pointed at a man who had raised his hand and challenged him: "If you really believe—get in!" There were no takers. God says to get in if we mean business.

A man fell off a cliff but managed to grab a tree limb on the way down. The following conversation ensued:

"Is anyone up there?"

"I am here. I am the Lord. Do you believe in me?"

"Yes, Lord, I believe. I really believe, but I can't hang on much longer."

"That's all right. If you really believe you have nothing to
    worry about, I will save you. Just let go of the branch."
A moment of pause, then: "Is anyone else up there?"

Are you committed to living by faith, or are you merely talking about faith? Faith is in us, but it must be released, and that
is done by praying, saying, and taking action. Prayer carries our
faith-filled requests before the throne of God and He answers.
Pray boldly, for He is able to do more than we can imagine (Ephesians 3:20, Hebrews 4:16).

What is in your heart will come out of your mouth. Pay attention to what you are saying, and it will often help you discover
how much faith you truly have. A man or woman of faith can still
speak positively about a situation even when the circumstances
have not changed. A person may have listened to hundreds of
Bible teachings on faith, but I can tell whether or not they truly
have faith just by listening to them for a little while. Words in
agreement with God's Word will release faith and allow it to go
to work in the supernatural realm.

Taking action releases faith. When I sit at the computer and
put my hands on the keys I am taking action. I am releasing my
faith and God shows up. That would not work for someone who
has no gift to write, but even though I do have a gift, I still must
begin and in faith continue throughout the process.

When Peter got out of the boat, his action proved that he had
faith in God's Word when he heard Jesus say, "Come." Is God
asking you to do something and you're waiting to feel safe? If
so, that isn't faith. In order to do or have greater things, we are
usually required to let go of what we have and head into the

unknown. God told Abraham to leave his country, his home, and his relatives and go to a land that God would show him after he started on his way. He had to leave, not knowing where he was going. That is faith!

The Faith for Daily Life

The type of faith we have been talking about is required for new challenges and tasks greater than those we have confronted previously. But there is also the type of faith that we need for daily living—faith to pay the bills, keep a good job, raise the kids, make marriage work, get along with people, etc. Faith for daily living is vital if we are going to eliminate stress and enjoy life. The faith habit will leave no room for the worry habit. It also drives out the fear habit. Developing a habit of simply trusting God in every situation will help you overcome many other bad habits.

Verbalize your faith. Say frequently, "I trust God." Or "I believe that God is working in my life and circumstances right now." We speak out of faith, but then what we say also increases our faith. In the Bible, David said, "I will say of the Lord, He is my Refuge and my Fortress, my God; on Him I lean *and* rely, *and* in Him I [confidently] trust!" (Psalm 91:2).

The best way to defeat worry and fear is to resist them right away when they first try to enter your mind. The apostle Peter said that we should resist the devil at his onset (I Peter 5:9). Lift up the shield of faith, and with it you can extinguish all the fiery darts of the evil one (Ephesians 6:16). Developing the faith habit will shield you from many negative and tormenting emotions. We can learn to live by faith (Romans 1:17).

Faith is filled with hopeful expectation and it never gives up. Someone has rightly said, "When faith goes to market, it always takes a basket." Keep your basket handy because God may fill it at any moment.

Faith for the Past

We can have faith today that takes care of all of our past mistakes and failures. Regret over yesterday can ruin today unless we live by faith. The devil wants us to think that we cannot overcome our past or that it is too late for us to have a good life, but he is a liar. God's Word teaches us to let go of the past by faith and press toward the things that are ahead. If you are concerned about something from your past, meditate on this Scripture and let it encourage you to trust God.

> Behold, I am doing a new thing! Now it springs forth; do you not perceive *and* know it *and* will you not give heed to it? I will even make a way in the wilderness and rivers in the desert.
>
> *Isaiah 43:19*

The reality of this Scripture can be yours by simply releasing your faith and believing that no matter what has happened in the past, God is greater than your past. He will forgive your sins, turn your mistakes into miracles, and leave you amazed at the good things He will do in your life.

Faith for the Future

We all think we would love to know the future. People who don't know how to trust God may spend thousands of dollars consulting fortune-tellers and supposed psychics hoping to get a glimpse into the future. They don't need to waste their money. God is the only One who knows the future. He might choose to speak of the future through one of His prophets, but usually He just wants us to trust Him. The "What am I going to do?" question is frequently on all of our minds, but we don't have to entertain it. I don't know exactly what the future holds for me, but I do believe that whatever it is, it will be God's good and perfect plan. One Christian man often said, "I don't know what the future holds, but I do know Who holds the future."

Anytime a worry comes to our mind about the future, we can immediately choose faith in God instead of worry.

The world condition today is very unstable, and the pressure to worry about it is increasing. What if the economy totally fails? What if I lose my job and all my retirement savings? I drive a hundred miles round-trip daily to work, so what am I going to do if gasoline prices keep going up? I never had any children; who will take care of me when I am old? The questions and wonderings are endless if we let our minds go there, but we can also choose to develop the faith habit. We don't know all the answers, but we can know God, and He does know the answers. When faith is a habit, we won't waste our time and energy on worry.

You may have a situation looming in the future that you know you will need to confront, and you just don't feel that you are up to it. Don't worry. God will give you the grace, wisdom, and strength you need when the times comes. Until then, have faith!

The Journey from Fear to Faith

Our natural instinct is to be afraid and try to protect and take care of ourselves, but God invites us to a life of faith. Fear is tormenting. Sadly, sometimes people have lived in fear for so long that they don't realize it is abnormal. We can develop behavior systems that allow us to function in our dysfunction.

I had many fears in my life due to being raised in an abusive and dysfunctional home. I had learned to function with them, but as I studied the Word of God, I also learned that I did not have to live with them. I learned there was a better way—the way of faith. However, getting from fear to faith was and still is a journey. I was afraid of being rejected, displeasing people, and not being truly loved for myself. I feared what people thought of me. My reputation meant a lot to me. I feared failure, being wrong in choices I made, and being judged or criticized for my decisions and actions. I also feared my past mistakes, the unknown future, not having enough money to take care of myself, and needing to depend on someone else.

I can truly say that none of these fears prevail in my life now.

They may rear their ugly heads from time to time, but I am no longer controlled by them. I have developed the faith habit, and you can do it too.

Learning about and receiving the unconditional love of God is what sets us free from fear. Nothing else will! Perfect love casts out fear (1 John 4:18). Only God has perfect love, and it can be ours by faith. Take God at His word and begin to receive His love for you and allow Him to set you free from all fear. Faith works by love (Galatians 5:6). How can we put our trust in God if we are not convinced that He loves us at all times? Knowing and believing in God's love is one of the key ingredients in being able to live a life of faith.

Faith goes up the stairs that love has built and looks out the window which hope has opened.

Charles H. Spurgeon

The Bible says frequently, "Fear not, for I am with you." God is with you and has promised to never leave you or forsake you. You don't grow in faith by wishing that you felt a certain way or didn't feel a certain way, but you grow by stepping out and trusting the promises of God. Each time you do, you gain experience that will help you trust the next time. Don't be discouraged with yourself if it takes a while to develop the faith habit. I don't think anyone operates in perfect faith, but thankfully we can continue to grow. Aren't you glad that you don't have to feel pressured to manifest perfection in anything? Jesus Christ, the Perfect One, has paved the way for us, and we can follow one step at a time.

Remember this: God is pleased with you as long as you keep pressing on, and He is not disappointed with you because you are not perfect. Our faithlessness does not change God's faithfulness (2 Timothy 2:13).

Acceptance with Joy

The faith habit allows us to accept whatever our circumstances are with joy because we trust that God works all things out for good (Romans 8:28). We can trust God no matter what things look or feel like. Mrs. Charles E. Cowman, who wrote *Streams in the Desert*, said, "We must take God at His word. Experience reveals that such a faith will not make the sun shine sooner, but it will make the night seem shorter."

Trust is simply asking God for what you want, need, or desire and giving Him the respect and honor due Him by allowing Him to bring it to pass when and how He sees fit. God doesn't necessarily want to hear us asking why and when, but does love to hear us say, "I trust You."

God wants us to trust Him *in* things, and not merely *for* something. Our ways are not His ways, but His ways are perfect. His timing is not ours, but He is never late. The faith habit will help us maintain the happy habit.

> Whatever you ask for in prayer, believe (trust and be confident) that it is granted to you, and you will [get it].
>
> *Mark 11:24*

This Scripture is exciting, but we must realize that it does not tell us *when* we will get what we have asked for. We inherit the promises of God through faith and patience (Hebrews 6:12). Our impatience won't make God hurry, and we might as well decide to wait with joy. Acceptance with joy is proof of faith. Our attitude says loud and clear, "I believe God is perfect in all of His ways, and I know I am in His hands."

Abandon Yourself to God

Totally let go of trying to control your life and circumstances and trust God with everything. Abandonment is forgetting the past entirely, leaving the future completely in His hands, and being totally at peace with the present, knowing that the moment you are in contains God's perfect will for you for that moment. Watchman Nee, a powerful Chinese Christian who was martyred for his faith, including having his tongue cut out for preaching, died with this note under his pillow.

> Christ is the Son of God. He died to atone for men's sin, and after three days rose again. This is the most important fact in the universe. I die believing in Christ.
>
> *Watchman Nee*

He had the faith habit. Nothing could stop it, not even suffering and death. If we can learn to live with this kind of faith, all of life becomes a tremendous joy and we are at perfect rest as we wait on God.

10

Behavior 7: The Habit of Excellence

So that you may surely learn to sense what is
vital, *and* approve *and* prize what is excellent *and*
of real value...

Philippians 1:10

It is very easy to be a mediocre person. All you have to do is make no extra effort of any kind and drift through life making no difference in the world, which will guarantee that you leave no legacy behind when you are gone. You probably won't even be noticed or stand out because there are millions of other people who are also mediocre. But if you will dare to form the habit of being excellent in all that you do, you will be a bright light in the darkness, and that is exactly what God has called you to be.

God is excellent and we are created in His image; therefore, if we are to reach our full potential in Him we must also choose to be excellent. God has an excellent plan in mind for our lives, but a mediocre, lazy, and compromising person will not live in the fulfillment of an excellent destiny. We all have a choice to make about how we will live, and I believe God wants to use this book to urge you to make your choice if you haven't already done so. If you have already made your decision to be excellent, then use this as an opportunity to recommit, and keep pressing on.

Excellence is seen in doing the best you can in every situation, but it is not necessarily perfection. Excellence is extremely high quality and a virtue to be pursued. Edwin Bliss said, "The pursuit of excellence is gratifying and healthy. The pursuit of perfection is frustrating, neurotic, and a terrible waste of time." It is important that you see the difference between striving for excellence and striving for perfection. If you don't, you will be frustrated and feel like a failure every step of the way.

Did you know that most people who have the habit of procrastination are perfectionists? Because they feel compelled to do a perfect job and fear that they won't be able to achieve it, they put off the task. We tend to think that procrastinators are lazy, and maybe some are. But most are not lazy, they are fearful of falling below others' expectations.

It is actually a wonderful thing to realize that as human beings with flaws and weaknesses we rarely do all things perfectly or never make mistakes. That is the reason why God sent His Son as a perfect substitute for us. We should have an excellent attitude and desire in every situation to do the best we can do, and then trust God to do what we cannot do. I always say, "Do your best and trust God to do the rest!" If you do what you can do, then God will do what you cannot do.

Jesus told us to be perfect as our Father in heaven is perfect (Matthew 5:48). When I initially read that verse of Scripture, I felt pressured because I knew I could not be perfect. But I discovered by reading the Amplified Bible that the word *perfect* in the original Greek language means *to grow* into complete maturity of character. God wants us always to be growing and making progress, but He is never angry with us because we have not yet arrived. Even the apostle Paul said that although he pressed toward the mark of perfection, he had not yet arrived.

If we compromise it means that we do a little less than we know is right and proper, and to be excellent means to do a little more than you might have to in order to get by. It means to go the extra mile. There was a time in society when excellence was fairly normal, but that is not the case today. Our passion for more, which is greed, has driven us to prefer quantity instead of quality, and that is sad. Stephen R. Covey said, "Doing more things faster is no substitute for doing the right things."

When we had our home built we found out how difficult it is to find companies that have a commitment to excellence. When an appointment was not kept the excuse was always, "We are just so busy that we got behind and couldn't make it to your home." In other words, they had taken on more than they could do properly, and in the process they did very little with excellence, including keeping their word.

Making the commitment to being habitually excellent and following through on your commitments will be very rewarding. There is nothing about mediocrity that makes us feel good inside about ourselves or our choices.

Help Yourself

If you want to form a habit of being excellent, develop some kind of system to help you remember to press past the point of comfort. It is easy to vacuum in the middle of the room, but to do an excellent job you may have to get under the furniture and move a few things out of the way. Pressing into excellence won't be easy at first, but eventually it will become a habit and you won't be comfortable unless you do everything you do in the best way possible.

I am a big fan of signs or notes to help us remember while we are forming new habits. Make five signs that simply say EXCELLENCE and place them strategically where you will see them several times a day. I also strongly believe in the power of verbal confession to help us form a new image of ourselves, so try saying out loud at least ten times day, "I do what I do with excellence." Do that for a while and then expand your confession to "I am an excellent person, I do my work with excellence, I take excellent care of myself and all that I own, I treat people excellently, I think excellent thoughts, and I speak excellent words." The confessions you make, perhaps totally by faith in the beginning of your journey, will help you not only remember to do things with excellence, but they will change how you see yourself. Once you see yourself as being excellent, it will be no struggle to do what you do with excellence.

Remember that habits are developed through repetition. As you repeatedly choose the more excellent way in every situation, you will not only form the habit of excellence, you will break the habit of mediocrity.

Do Your Best for God

Excellence is to do a common thing in an uncommon way.

Booker T. Washington

Henry Kissinger, in his book *The White House Years*, tells of a Harvard professor who had given an assignment and now was collecting the papers. He handed them back the next day and at the bottom of one was written, "Is this the best you can do?" The student thought no and redid the paper. It was handed in again and received the same comment. This went on ten times, till finally the student said, "Yes, this is the best I can do." The professor replied, "Fine, now I'll read it." We know in our hearts if we are truly doing the best we can do. If we are not, then we should strive to do so.

It would seem obvious that there is no way we can love God with our heart, soul, mind, and strength (Mark 12:30) without seeking to do our very best to glorify God. The pursuit of excellence is a mark of maturity if we seek it with the right motive. Our motive should be to obey and glorify God and to represent Him well on earth. But a person can seek to be excellent merely out of his own obsession for significance, to be noticed and praised by others, or for worldly promotion. Let's do all that we do to glorify God, and He will reward us by giving us the other things that we desire.

When I began my own pursuit of excellence it was because God had challenged me to do so. In the beginning of my ministry, God spoke three things to my heart and impressed upon me that if I would do those things for Him, I would be successful. The first was to keep the strife out of my life, the second was to do all that I did with excellence, and the third was to be a person of integrity, being honest in all that I did. At that time the extent of my ministry was teaching a Bible study in my home, but I took the responsibility seriously and studied very hard each week for my lesson. I was also a wife and the mother of three children at that time. I was not able to drop everything and head off to Bible school or seminary, so God taught me in my daily life.

He taught me to always pick up after myself and never leave messes for someone else out of laziness. He taught me to put things back where I got them. God impressed on me to always put my grocery cart back where it belonged at the grocery store after unloading my groceries into the car. When I was shopping for clothing and knocked an item off the hanger onto the floor, He taught me that to be excellent, I had to pick it up and put it back on the hanger and not leave it for someone else to do. There were hundreds of seemingly little things like this that God dealt with me about during those years.

It was hard in the beginning, and one of the biggest excuses I used was that other people were not doing it, so why should I? God reminded me that I had asked Him to do great things in my life and then asked me if I really wanted them or not. He was in essence saying, "We reap what we sow." Don't ever be satisfied to be like everyone else, but instead choose to be the best you that you can be.

In some of these things I wrestled with my emotions for as much as two years before becoming fully obedient to God and developing the habit of being excellent. I learned that if we sow excellence, we will reap the most excellent reward. What do you want out of life? Are you willing to sow the right kind of seed to get it? Ask yourself some hard questions and give truthful answers.

Do you do what you do with excellence?

How often do you compromise and take the easy way out?

Do you drift along in life, or are you pressing toward the best?

Do you keep your commitments?

Do you always tell the truth?

Do you leave messes for other people to clean up?

If you accidentally get an item at the store that you didn't pay for, do you return it?

Do you put your grocery cart back in the space designated after you load your groceries into your car?

If you have put an item into your grocery cart and decide later that you really don't need it, do you put it back where you got it or just leave it anywhere to get rid of it?

I could keep adding to the list, but I think you get the point I am trying to make. We can never get to where we want to be unless we truthfully admit where we are right now. It is facing truth that makes us free.

The Rewards of Excellence

Every good choice brings a reward and, unfortunately, so does every bad choice. The rewards of excellence are wonderful. I recall a woman who told me she had listened to my teaching on excellence and integrity and that it had totally changed her approach to life. She said she'd had no teaching in this area previously and had no idea how mediocre and subpar she was. She thanked me and said, "It was challenging at first, but becoming excellent has changed my whole life."

When we are excellent, we feel better about ourselves. We have confidence that we are doing what God would want us to do. We become a good example to other people. This is especially important for parents to model in front of their children. It is important for those who are in leadership of any kind to set this example for all those under their authority.

A woman sent in this testimony regarding how her decision to be excellent affected her.

Dear Joyce,

Just a testimony of how God gave me the "opportunity" to apply your teaching this morning on television, to a situation in my life this afternoon. This was in regard to your talking about how God dealt with you about being excellent and always cleaning up your messes.

I was taking out my recycling cans and glasses to the community receptacle, and as I went to open the lid, the paper bag in my hand ripped and a glass jar dropped to the cement floor and shattered. I was real tempted to pick up the big pieces and leave the little dangerous mess. All sorts of excuses immediately raced through my mind. "I shouldn't leave the baby alone. I'm so tired. I have a broom, but I don't know where the dustpan is. It is hot outside." However, your teaching was too fresh in my mind; so I told my feet to take my flesh back up to my apartment to get the broom and dustpan and clean up my mess.

The nice thing about cleaning up the mess was the freedom of just forgetting about the whole thing once I chose the more excellent way.

Her excellence was rewarded with peace in her heart. I think peace is one of the greatest rewards we receive when we make an effort to do things the way we know they should be done and don't compromise and do a little less than we know is right. It is wonderful not to feel condemned by what we allow ourselves to do. Sometimes the feelings of guilt or lack of peace are vague, but they are nonetheless present and they disturb our freedom.

The name Stradivarius is synonymous with fine violins. This is because Antonio Stradivari insisted that no instrument constructed in his shop be sold until it was as near perfection (excellence) as human skill and care could make it. Stradivari observed, "God needs violins to send His music into the world, and if any violins are defective God's music will be spoiled." His work philosophy was summed up in one sentence: "Other men will make other violins, but no man shall make a better one."

Stradivari had a commitment to excellence because he wanted to do his best for God. His reward is that his violins are still known worldwide today as being the best.

Excellence in Our Thoughts

We can never become excellent in our actions if we don't first make a commitment to become excellent in our thoughts. The Bible teaches us to think on things that are filled with virtue and excellence (Philippians 4:8). Things like believing the best at all times, things that are honorable, just, pure, lovely, and lovable. I talk about our thoughts in all of my books and most of my messages because of their importance. We become what we allow our thoughts to be (Proverbs 23:7).

What kind of thoughts do you entertain? When you recognize that your thoughts are not good, do you take action to cast them out of your mind, or do you lazily let them remain? It is impossible to become an excellent person without first developing an excellent mind.

Don't make the mistake of thinking that your thoughts don't matter because nobody knows them anyway. They do matter and God knows them. Wrong thoughts can poison our lives and attitudes. Since they are the forerunner to all of our words and actions, we must deal with them first. You can think what you want to think. You are in control, and even though Satan will try to put wrong and deadly thoughts in your mind, you can cast them out and choose right ones. Your mind and thoughts belong to you, and you should not allow the devil to use your mind as a garbage dump or you will end up with a stinking mess of a life.

Excellence in Speech

The psalmist David says, in Proverbs 8:6, "Hear, for I will speak excellent *and* princely things; and the opening of my lips shall be for right things." He was making a decision about how he would talk and we should do the same thing. Just as we can direct our thoughts, we can also direct our words with God's help. The power of life and death are in the tongue, and we eat the fruit of them (Proverbs 18:21). Our words affect us and the people around us. They also affect what God is able to do for us. We cannot have a negative mouth and a positive life.

The apostle Peter teaches us that if we want to enjoy life and see good days even in the midst of trials, we must keep our tongue free from evil (1 Peter 3:10). To me this Scripture says something extremely important that we want to pay attention to. What kind of life do you want? Do you want an excellent life? If so, then you must develop the habit of being excellent in your choice of words.

We cannot merely say whatever we feel like saying, but we must choose our words carefully because they are containers for power. They can carry creative or destructive power, and the choice is up to us. The tongue is a tiny organ, but it can cause great trouble or bring great blessings. Change your words and your life will change!

As far as I am concerned, it is a privilege to understand the power of words. I spent the first thirty-five years of my life not having any idea that what I said made any difference to the quality of my life. Your words and mine affect us in greater ways than we can possibly imagine, and we are challenged in Scripture to let them be excellent.

Make it a habit to say nothing if you cannot say something that is worth saying.

Treat People with Excellence

Finally, let me say that it is important that we learn to treat all people excellently. God loves all people and does not take it kindly when we mistreat anyone. Be polite, respectful, and appreciative. Be encouraging! Everyone in the world wants to feel valuable, and many are struggling with feelings of low self-esteem. We are in a position to be used by God to help them by treating all people with excellence.

The apostle Paul teaches that we are to pursue love and that it is the most excellent way to live.

> But earnestly desire *and* zealously cultivate the greatest *and* best gifts *and* graces (the higher gifts and the choicest graces). And yet I will show you a still more excellent way [one that is better by far and the highest of them all—love].
>
> *1 Corinthians 12:31*

11

Behavior 8: The Habit of Being Responsible

Ninety-nine percent of all failure comes from people
who have a habit of making excuses.

George Washington Carver

Making excuses each time we are faced with taking responsibility for some action or lack of action is a very bad habit. It can
easily derail our life and will likely prevent success. If we take
responsibility for our lives, it can often be a shocking experience,
because suddenly we have no one to blame. Jesus said that many
are called and few are chosen (Matthew 20:16). I think that may
mean that although many are called to do great things for God,
few are willing to take the responsibility for their call. Being
responsible is what makes us honorable people. It is the price of
greatness, according to Sir Winston Churchill.

Excuses are nothing new. They have been used by humans

to avoid responsibility since time began. After Adam and Eve sinned in the Garden of Eden, they both made excuses when confronted by God. They both blamed others. Adam blamed Eve and God for giving him Eve, and Eve blamed the devil. People make excuses for their sins all the time instead of simply admitting them, confessing them, and asking God to forgive them. Taking full responsibility for our actions is possibly one of the most emotionally painful things that we face in life. We desperately want to think we are good, and we feel that to fully admit we have made a mistake and not done what we should have done spoils our goodness. We all have things to face about ourselves, and it is a brave man or woman who is willing to do it. We should never be afraid to admit that we are wrong about something or that we have made a mistake. The truth is what sets us free (John 8:32). Avoiding, evading, and making excuses keeps us in bondage.

Because the truth makes us free, our enemy the devil will fill our heads with excuses and ways to blame other people and things for our shortcomings. He knows that we will remain trapped in our problems if we refuse to take responsibility for our actions.

Take the example of being late. When people are late for an appointment or for work they rarely simply say, "I'm sorry I am late. I didn't manage my time well and I didn't leave my house when I should have." Instead we say things like, "I'm late because I got caught in traffic. I didn't know I needed to get gasoline. My kids were being impossible and my husband misplaced my car keys." That may well be true occasionally, but when it happens all the time, there is a definite problem that needs to be addressed. Even if some of those things did happen, it was still our responsibility to leave early enough to accommodate for traffic, to make sure we had gasoline or time to get it, and to manage our households well enough to avoid the other issues.

Did you know that when you're late, you are sending the message that your time is more valuable than the person's who is waiting for you? At the very least, call that person and tell her you're running late and when you expect to arrive. That is being responsible!

Making an excuse for being late is minor compared to all the excuses that people make for an endless list of things. But excuses are never pleasing to God because He loves the truth and wants us to love it too. Making excuses can easily fall into the category of lies, and that causes us to break the commandment "Thou shalt not lie."

When we make excuses we are actually lying to ourselves as well as others. We are keeping ourselves in deception through reasoning. We can easily find a reason for every error, but it is better to simply take responsibility for our actions.

There are, of course, reasons why things happen, and sharing those reasons is not always a problem unless we are using them as an excuse to not change. I love it when I hear someone say, "I take full responsibility for that mistake." It immediately causes me to respect and trust them.

People in the Bible Who Made Excuses

Jesus tells a parable of a man giving a great supper who invited many to come, but they all began to make excuses. One said he had purchased a piece of land and had to go out and see it. Another said he bought some farm animals and needed to go examine them, and another said he had gotten married and because of that he was unable to come. All of these excuses were just that—excuses. The truth was that they didn't want to come. This parable is representative of God inviting people into a relationship with Him and all the excuses they make when the truth is that they don't want to. They want to run their own lives, even though they are doing it badly, and they don't want God interfering.

Even among those who are believers in Jesus we hear ample excuses for not serving Him fully. People don't have enough time; they are busy working or running their children back and forth to sporting events. What we do with our time is a matter of choice, and the truth is that we do what we really want to do. If we want to do a thing strongly, then we find time for it. There is one truth that none of us will be able to avoid. The day will come when every person will stand before God and give an account of their lives (Romans 14:12). On that day there will be no excuses.

Moses made excuses when God called him to service. He said that he wasn't eloquent enough and could not speak. God finally became angry with all of his excuses. King Saul made excuses about why he didn't fully obey God by completely destroying the Amalekites. Felix made excuses when Paul was speaking to him about righteousness and self-control. He said, "Go away and come back at a more convenient time." The road to hell is paved with the good intentions of those who made excuses for not doing the right thing now but said they intended to do it later.

Peter may have had many excuses in his mind for denying

Christ. I doubt that he simply said to himself, "I am a coward." We all make excuses, but it is time to deal with them and form a habit of being responsible.

Integrity

Integrity is vitally important. It is part of being an excellent person. People of integrity take responsibility for their actions. They keep their commitments instead of making excuses for not keeping them. They keep their promises. They do what they tell people they are going to do, and if for some reason they absolutely cannot, then they contact the person, give an explanation—not an excuse—and ask to be released from the commitment.

We expect God to keep His promises, and He expects us to keep ours. Some people today don't even know what the word *integrity* means. It should be taught in schools and colleges, and if it were, we would have more people in the world with good character. As I mentioned earlier, God told me that if I wanted to be a success in ministry, then I must be a person of integrity. To us at Joyce Meyer Ministries, this has been a top priority. I know there have been times when we have not been able to do what we said we would do, but it was never intentional. I have learned over the years to be more careful about the commitments I make. When we make them rashly or emotionally, we often end up wishing we hadn't made them at all and sometimes find that we cannot keep them. Be very careful when you give your word that you will do something. It is better to not commit at all than to commit and then make an excuse for not following through. Don't even tell someone that you will call them back on the phone unless you intend to do so.

Traits of a Responsible Person

When a person is committed to being responsible, you can count on them to be dependable. They finish what they start and do what they say they will do. They rarely give up on anything because they are steadfast and dedicated.

Responsible people pay their bills on time. They think ahead and don't spend more money than they earn. If they do fall on hard times, they don't ignore their responsibilities, but they are truthful with those they are committed to and make arrangements to make things right as soon as they can.

Responsible people don't have to worry about the future, because they have planned ahead. They have prepared for the future by saving a portion of what they earn for emergencies or retirement. In Proverbs chapter 31, we meet a woman who is the perfect example of what a responsible person looks like. She gets up before sunrise to plan for the day. She works hard, and although she wants to expand, she always seriously considers whether expanding would be prudent. She spends time with God so she is strong for whatever life may bring. She helps the poor and needy. She doesn't fear bad weather because she has already made proper clothing for her family.

Responsible people take good care of what they own. They are good stewards of what God has blessed them with. They take care of themselves because they know their life and health are gifts from God that they need to protect. They take care of family obligations, including meeting the needs of elderly parents or grandparents. When they have a job that needs to be done, they do it. They do it without having to be prodded or reminded multiple times. They are self-motivated, and that means they don't need outside influence to make them do what they should be doing.

I believe that helping the poor and those who are less fortunate than we are is not only a nice thing to do but is our responsibility. The Bible teaches us not to forget them.

He who despises his neighbor sins [against God, his fellowman, and himself], but happy (blessed and fortunate) is he who is kind *and* merciful to the poor.

Proverbs 14:21

Helping people who are hurting is not something we can do or not do depending on how we happen to feel at the time; it is something God has commanded us to do. It is our responsibility. Anyone who has anything is responsible to help someone who has less than they do.

I have been blessed with a responsible nature, and I have seen the benefit and rewards of it in my life. My brother, who is now deceased, was not responsible, and I can honestly say that his entire life was one big mess after another. I loved him, but he was lazy, mediocre, and irresponsible. He had every opportunity in front of him that anyone could have had, but he wanted others to do for him what he should have been doing for himself.

Everyone who is successful is also responsible. Success and personal responsibility cannot be separated.

It doesn't matter how many opportunities we have in life if we won't be responsible to do what we need to do to take advantage of them. I boldly ask you to examine your life truthfully. Are you a responsible individual? Are there areas in which you could improve? Do you make excuses when you do something wrong? Are you defensive when you are corrected? As I said, facing truth is often emotionally painful, but it is one of the most powerful and freeing things that we can do. If you don't already have the habit of being responsible, are you willing to start right now developing it?

Responsible people do not have to feel like doing the right thing in order to do it. They cease asking themselves how they feel early in life because they know there will be times when they won't feel like doing what they should be doing, and they have already decided not to let how they feel make their decisions. When a mother has young children, she must take care of them no matter how she feels. She doesn't even consider not taking care of them because she knows that she must do it. We should look at more of our responsibilities like that. Let's stop seeing our responsibilities as options and instead see them as things that we must do.

Five Steps to Stop Making Excuses

Face the truth

The first step in dealing with any bad habit is to admit that you have a problem. Don't put off confronting it, hoping it will go away on its own. Everyone else knows that you are just making excuses, and it is time that you knew it too. **State your problem out loud**. Say it to God, say it to yourself, and it may even be helpful to tell a trusted friend. The apostle James said that we are to confess our faults to one another that we might be healed and restored (James 5:16).

Don't have unrealistic expectations

Before you make any commitment—even a small one—ask yourself if you truly believe you can and will follow through. Some people set unrealistic goals and they always fail. A little bit of forethought could have saved them lots of trouble. Be realistic about how long it takes to do things, and allow yourself enough time to do them without being stressed out about them. If you need to say no to a request, don't hesitate to do so. We are responsible to follow God's expectations of us, not everyone else's.

Stop complaining

As long as we complain about the things we need to do, we are likely to find excuses not to do them. Complaining about a task actually drains our energy to do it. If you want to exercise, don't complain all the time about how hard it is. Just do it. The Israelites complained about many things, and they remained in the wilderness for forty long years. Complaining keeps us from making progress.

Be aggressive

Don't procrastinate in taking care of your responsibilities. It is often best to do the things first that you like the least. That way you have no time to dread them, and you can do them while you have the most energy. Approach them aggressively, and don't let a lethargic attitude take over. If you put something off too long, you will get tired from other activities and find yourself making an excuse for not taking care of your main responsibility.

Find a solution to obstacles

Instead of complaining and making excuses for not doing something, use your energy to find a solution to your obstacle so you can more easily take care of your responsibility. If you're late for work frequently and it frustrates you because traffic is heavy, think about leaving earlier. Years ago, Dave worked at a company that was far from our home. He got to work half an hour early just so he would miss the heavy traffic. He used that time to study and read. We can find a solution to most problems if we truly want to.

No Excuses, Just Results

At the gym where I exercise they sell shirts that say "No Excuses, Just Results." Any time I even start to murmur, my coach says, "No excuses, just results." They know how apt people are to make excuses of all kinds for not being at the gym regularly.

Some of the exercises are very hard, and it is tempting to make excuses not to do them.

Our flesh has an aversion to thinking that there is no excuse for not meeting our responsibility, but if we truly want to succeed in life, we must learn to believe that and practice it. If we make excuses and blame others for our mistakes, we give up our power to change. Truth is a powerful weapon, and when faced squarely, it will help you become the person you say you want to be.

12

Behavior 9: The Habit of Generosity

> It is well with the man who deals generously and
> lends, who conducts his affairs with justice.
>
> *Psalm 112:5*

No Strings Attached!

One of the bad habits we should want to break is being selfish and self-centered, and the best way to do that is to form the habit of being generous. Generosity makes one's soul truly beautiful. God is generous, and all those who wish to be like Him must learn to be generous. I once heard that when we give we are more like God than at any other time.

When something is a habit, we actually miss it if we are not doing it. We should have such a strong habit of generosity that we actually crave the opportunity to do things for others. We can and should form a habit of being generous. That means that we choose to do more than we would have to do, and always do as much as we possibly can. We should never be the type of person who only does what they absolutely have to do, and even then does it with murmuring and complaining. God delights in a person with a willing and a generous heart. He loves a cheerful giver (2 Corinthians 9:7).

I don't enjoy it at all when someone does something for me and I can sense that they resent doing it. It actually ruins the whole thing, and I would rather that they not do it at all. My father was not a generous man. As a matter of fact, I don't ever remember him doing anything for anyone unless there was something in it for him. He even told me repeatedly that nobody really cared about anyone else, and everyone was out to get something. I am sure he believed that because that was the way he was, but how sad to live your whole life with that kind of attitude. Any time my father did anything for anyone there was always something he wanted in return. The truth is, that type of giving isn't real giving at all. When people give with that kind of attitude, they are in reality purchasing something. We often hear that we should give with no strings attached, which means to give expecting nothing in return. We should give generously, not expecting anything from the one we give to, but knowing that God blesses and rewards the generous person.

> The merciful, kind, *and* generous man benefits himself [for his deeds return to bless him], but he who is cruel *and* callous [to the wants of others] brings on himself retribution.
>
> *Proverbs 11:17*

I can still remember how much I hated it when my father let me go to a movie or borrow his car and yet made me feel guilty for doing it. It was a terrible feeling, and I don't want to ever make anyone feel that way. I don't believe we are being truly generous unless we do what we do with a willing heart. Giving may begin as a discipline, but it should develop into a desire. We can learn to give for the sheer joy we find in doing it.

A spirit of generosity causes a person to give even when it seems unreasonable to do so. The apostle Paul speaks of the generosity of the churches in Macedonia. Even though they were experiencing an ordeal of severe tribulation and deep poverty, they had so much joy that it overflowed in lavish generosity. They gave according to their ability, and even beyond their ability (what would have been comfortable) (2 Corinthians 8:2–3). Just reading about these people makes me admire them and want to be like them. We are drawn to generous people, and we instinctively don't want to be in the presence of a stingy person for very long.

Generosity Is the Answer to Greed

Greed has become a huge problem in our society today. I am sure it has always been a problem, but the abundance of things that are available today makes it even more of a problem. Greed causes a person to never be satisfied or appreciative for very long no matter how much they have. The apostle Paul tells us that he had learned how to be content whether he had a lot or a little (Philippians 4:12). That lesson would be a valuable one for all people today.

Greed steals the life of the greedy person, because he can never be satisfied. Greedy people cannot enjoy what they do have because they are never genuinely content. It is not wrong to want things. God has either created or given us the ability to create many beautiful and needful things, and I believe He wants His children to enjoy them. But He wants us to enjoy them with a proper attitude. That attitude should be one of gratitude, contentment, and a willingness to be generous to others.

We must fight against greed, and the best way I know to do that is to develop the habit of generosity. Greed is such a huge problem that God's Word instructs us to not even associate with anyone who is known to be guilty of greed. Why would He say that? I believe it is because greed is a wicked spirit, and God doesn't want us to be affected by it. God wants us to grow in generosity, not in greed. We can easily be affected by the people we are around, especially if we have close association with them. If you want to be a generous person, make friends with other generous people. Watch how they live and learn from their example.

I am thinking of some people I often eat with who are always very friendly, encouraging, and kind to all the workers in the restaurant. They have a good attitude even if their meal isn't exactly what they expected, and they tip generously. Their entire attitude is one of generosity. Being with them helps make a meal very pleasant, and I am challenged by their behavior to always keep growing in generosity. Choose friends who make you a better person. Of course, we want to always reach out to people who need us to be an example to them, too, but it isn't good if those are the only kind of people we are around.

Be Generous on Purpose

People who are not in the habit of being generous may have to force themselves to be generous for a period of time, but I can assure you that after a while they will become addicted to it. Make a decision to be more of a blessing to others, and start looking for opportunities. When you hear of a person in need, don't think, "Somebody needs to help them," without asking God if you're the somebody He wants to use.

I love to give in a variety of ways, and I know many other people who feel the same way. We didn't start out that way but learned it by being in relationship with God and studying His Word. I was also affected by being with generous people who became an example to me. Initially, I had to begin being generous on purpose, but eventually I started actually loving it. My executive assistant says that she was one of the stingiest people alive, and she is now a radical, outrageous giver. She says that the greatest and most life-changing lesson she has learned from my teachings is to give. To transition from being that stingy to now being very generous, she had to begin by doing acts of generosity on purpose.

Our children have told Dave and me that one of the best things we taught them was to give. Learn to be generous and teach it to other people. If your spirit is agreeing with what you're reading here about generosity but you know that you are not a truly generous person, you can become one. Pray and ask God to help, and then just start doing things for people until it becomes a habit.

Don't think that you have to have a lot of money to be generous. Generosity can be practiced no matter how much or little you have. If you share what you have with others freely, you are a generous person. You may share a meal, give a helping hand, give hospitality by inviting others into your home, or you may give the gift of true friendship. I do like to give gifts to people, but things are not the only or even the most important thing to give.

The main thing should be that we are letting an abundance of good things flow out from us to others. Greed frightens me because I believe it can easily take hold of anyone if they don't fight against it. When God begins to bless us, the last thing we should do is get greedy. When blessings flow to us, that is the time to press in to being a blessing to others more than ever.

I will bless you [with abundant increase of favors] and make your name famous *and* distinguished, and you will be a blessing [dispensing good to others].

Genesis 12:2

God told Abraham that He intended to abundantly bless him, but the promise came with an instruction to be a blessing to others. If we become "keepers" of all that comes to us and we don't let it flow through us, we become like stopped-up wells. We have what is necessary to help people, but we refuse to let it flow out. Not only are others deprived of blessings if we are stingy or greedy, but we are very miserable. Do you possess your possessions, or do your possessions possess you? Are you able to use what you have to be a blessing? God is a giver, and if we want to enjoy life and fulfill our purpose, then we must become givers also.

There is a difference between one who occasionally gives and a giver. When a person occasionally gives, it is something they do, but when they become a giver, it is who they are. Giving has become a habit, and it is part of their character. They don't have to be convinced to give, they don't resent giving or secretly wish they did not have to do it, but instead they actually love giving and are always on the lookout for ways to do it.

This is a good place to stop for a moment and do a reality check. It is time for a truth test. Are you a generous giver? Do you give as much as you can in a variety of ways, or are you still holding back out of fear, trying very hard to make sure that you are taken care of first? If you know in your heart that you're not a generous person, don't feel guilty, but start developing a habit of being generous.

Make a Plan

What are some steps you can take to start forming this wonderful habit? I first suggest that you make a plan. Every day, think about people you can bless and in what ways you can bless them. The more you think of others, the less time you will have to concentrate on yourself and your own problems. I have discovered over the years that the less I think about myself, the happier I am.

Think of the people you will be with today, and then think about what their needs may be. Perhaps they just need encouragement. Perhaps they need to talk and you could bless them by listening. Perhaps they are in need financially and you could give them a gift certificate to the grocery store or a gas card. There are endless ways to bless people if we will just put our mind to it. If you don't know what the person needs, then begin listening to them, and it won't be long before you will hear them mention something they are lacking. A person might say, "I have been so discouraged lately," and that is your opportunity to encourage them. Or they could say in conversation, "I really need some new clothes, but I will have to wait awhile," you could consider buying them a new outfit. If they are the same size as you, you could give them some of yours. At times I have kept a list of things I have heard various people say that they want or need, and even if I can't do it for them right away, I keep it on my list and do it when I can. Learn to listen.

Another thing we can do is take an inventory of what we own that we don't use at all and start giving it away. There are always people who desperately need or want what we have and are not even using. My motto is "Use it or lose it."

We don't have to personally know a person to be a blessing to them. If we decide to be a blessing everywhere we go, that will have to include strangers. I have found that it makes people feel good if I ask their name when they are helping me in a store or restaurant. People want and need to feel that we are genuinely interested in them as an individual.

Plan to put smiles on faces. You can even start with a goal such as "I want to put a smile on at least one face a day"—that is, by being a blessing in some way. When you reach that goal consistently, raise it to two faces and then more and more. Soon generosity will become a lifestyle.

Be creative and pray for God to show you ways to be able to bless people. The more generous you become, the more you will be blessed in your own life. Do it for the glory of God and in obedience to Him. We cannot outgive God. He said if we give, it will be given back to us, pressed down, shaken together, and running over (Luke 6:38). You won't end up with less if you're a generous giver; you will actually prosper in all you do.

Generosity is not only giving ourselves and our money and things. It also involves how we treat people. Generous-spirited people will be patient with the weaknesses of others, quick to forgive, and slow to get angry. They always believe the best of people. They listen when others are hurting and make an attempt to provide comfort—or just show concern. They are also encouraging, and they build people up and edify them. They make a big deal out of what others do right but often don't even mention what they do wrong. If I had to choose between the two, I would rather have someone give me those things than pay for my lunch.

Creatures of Habit

We are creatures of habit, but bad habits can be broken and they can be replaced with good habits. As I have said already, I believe if we concentrate on forming good habits, the bad ones won't have any room to operate in our lives. We can form the habit of being a generous person who continually reaches out to others to make their lives better, and in doing so the bad habits we previously had will find no place in us. I admit that I was a very selfish, self-centered person for much of my life. We don't have to learn to be selfish. We are born with that ability. Thankfully, through the new birth in Jesus Christ, we can change. Jesus died so that we no longer have to live to and for ourselves (2 Corinthians 5:15). That is good news! We can be free from selfishness. We can be free from constantly thinking, "What about me?" We won't have to fear that our needs won't be met, because God will always take care of our needs when we busy ourselves with taking care of the needs of other people.

13

Behavior 10: The Hurry Habit

The devil has a hand in what is done in haste.

Turkish proverb

Busy people often feel they must hurry to get everything done they need to do, but I believe that if we must constantly hurry to get it all done, we are doing too much. Most people today say they have too much to do and lament the stress they are under, but they forget they made their schedule, and they are the only ones who can change it. Do we really have to do all the things that we do, or could we easily eliminate a few of them and be able to slow down and live life at a pace that could be enjoyed? I think we all know the answer to that question. Of course we can do less if we truly want to.

When we see the span of a person's life in print or on a tombstone, it starts with the year of their birth and ends with the year of their death. The only thing in between those two dates is a dash. Perhaps the dash is there because that is what our life seems like. We dash through everything, and before we know it, life is coming to an end and we may not have enjoyed it at all.

> Most men pursue pleasure with such breathless haste that they hurry past it.
>
> *Søren Kierkegaard*

Much of what we hurry to do is done because we think if we do it at that moment, we will enjoy life at some time in the future. I suggest we slow down and begin to enjoy life now!

Is God in a Hurry?

My experience is that God is not in a hurry. He seems to take His time about everything. He is not late, but He usually isn't early, and He expects us to be patient while we wait. Right now I am looking through a large glass door at trees, grass, flowers, and white birds that fly through the area occasionally. As I look, I realize that nature is not in a hurry, yet everything is accomplished that needs to be done.

People who enjoy being outside say they like nature because it is peaceful. I like it because it reminds me of God and His creation. I love the peace it brings. A leisurely walk through nature is helpful to our soul as well as our body. But how often do we take the time to do it? Some people walk or run for exercise, and they may enjoy the benefit they get from it, but that is quite different from walking just to enjoy God's creation and the peace it brings. Make a decision not to hurry past God's creation and never take time to notice, enjoy, and appreciate it.

For the past several years I have made an effort to learn how to enjoy everything that I do, and in order to do that I have to keep reminding myself to slow down. I might be referred to as a quick person. I make quick decisions, I move from one thing to another quickly, and occasionally I am moving so fast that I don't remember what I did. My daughter teasingly has asked me to wait until she parks the car to take off my seat belt and open the door to get out. If we are shopping together I can be in the store while she is still getting out of the car. If I don't keep reminding myself to slow down, I find my mind is usually one step ahead of where I am.

Dave rarely hurries, my son-in-law rarely hurries, and I do know a few other people like them, but most people are in a hurry, and sadly they are not even sure where they are headed in life. If you and I want to break the hurry habit, we will have to make changes in our lifestyle and mind-set. Good habits drive out bad ones; therefore, focus on staying peaceful and patient and hurry will eventually be a thing of the past.

Set an Overload Alarm

You really don't have to do everything that everyone wants you to do, and it is perfectly acceptable to say no. Protect your peace by refusing to overload your schedule. As soon as you start feeling pressured to do more than you know you can do peacefully, let that be your overload alarm. Just as an alarm clock signals us to get up and start the day, let your overload alarm be your signal to say no to whatever you must in order to remain peaceful. One of the people I have to say no to is myself. Sometimes I want to do things myself that cause me to feel pressured and I have to say, "Joyce, your peace is more important than this thing you want to do." Quite often we are our own worst enemy. We may want to be involved in everything that everyone we know is involved in, but it may not be best for us. If you follow wisdom, you can remain peaceful even when everyone you know is stressed from hurrying.

When making appointments that can quickly fill up all of your days, be sure to make appointments with yourself for rest and relaxation. Take time to evaluate your schedule often, and if there are things on it that are not bearing good fruit for you or that you no longer think you should be doing, eliminate them. Ask yourself if what you are doing is worth what you are doing to yourself in order to do it.

God is not in a hurry. If we hurry, we are likely to run right past Him and then wonder where He went. Learn to live in God's divine rhythm. Live at a pace that allows you to do what you do patiently and peacefully.

St. Francis de Sales said, "Never be in a hurry; do everything quietly and in a calm spirit. Do not lose your inner peace for anything whatsoever, even if your whole world seems upset."

The Benefits of Hurrying

As I ponder what the benefits of hurrying are, I honestly cannot think of any. But I can quickly think of several disadvantages. Continual hurrying is bad for our health. It places stress on us, and we all know what that does. Hurrying harms our relationships. We either never take time to develop any, or if we do have friends, we don't take time to truly listen to them or meet their needs. We often ignore our family in the pursuit of accomplishing all the things we have to do. We are too busy to listen to the kids when they try to tell us something, too busy to visit our elderly parents who are lonely, and too busy to put time into our marriage that will surely fall apart someday if we don't. I have already mentioned one of the huge disadvantages of hurrying, and that is that we don't enjoy anything we are doing. Life goes by in a blur, and at the end of it we will regret that we didn't do less and enjoy it more.

In fact, I daresay that many of the things we regarded as a waste of our time will be the very things that we treasure most in years to come. How many mothers do you know with grown children who would give anything to be able to sit with their little child and be regaled with every single thing that happened that day? How many wives would love nothing more than to watch endless reruns of old *Star Trek* episodes with their husband—if only he were there. How many of us will regret the times that we didn't call our mom just to say hi or drop by for a brief visit?

Every time we do one of those things, we are adding to our bank account. That account is not comprised of dollars to spend in later years. It is comprised of memories that we can enjoy over and over in the future.

Being in a hurry causes us to miss the truly important things in life. It makes us grouchy, impatient with people and things, and quick to display anger, and our excuse is always that we are busy and in a hurry, as if that pardons our wrong behavior. Impatience is merely internal hurry. We have to continually think and plan to try to get everything done we think we need to do. We are rushing in our soul, and when anyone or anything isn't moving as fast as we are, we display an impatient attitude.

For example, if I am in a hurry and Dave wants to tell me about the ball game from the night before, something I am not all that interested in anyway, I will almost always get impatient with him. Or if I am in a hurry and something mechanical isn't working the way it should, I feel very irritated and impatient and often find myself yelling at a hunk of metal. Have you ever become angry with your computer or cell phone and called it stupid? I have. I urge you to slow down and break the hurry habit before you do damage to yourself, the people around you, and the good plan that God has for you.

So many people hurry today that we may not even realize it is abnormal, but it is. It was never God's intention for us to rush through anything and have our soul in knots due to the stress of hurrying. Hurry is a peace-stealer, and one of the most precious gifts Jesus has left us is His peace. Without it, life is not worth living as far as I am concerned.

> Peace I leave with you; My [own] peace I now give *and* bequeath to you. Not as the world gives do I give to you. Do not let your hearts be troubled, neither let them be afraid. [Stop allowing yourselves to be agitated and disturbed; and do not permit yourselves to be fearful and intimidated and cowardly and unsettled.]
>
> *John 14:27*

The message in this verse of Scripture is clear. Jesus has left us His peace, but we must be responsible to arrange our lives in such a way that we can enjoy it. It is a gift Jesus has given freely, but we can totally miss the benefits of it unless we value it greatly. What could you change in your life that would immediately give you more peace?

If we know what to do and don't do it, then there is nothing that can be done to help us. We often pray for peace, but are we doing our part? God doesn't do everything for us, but He will show us what to do and then give us the ability to do it if we are willing. Once we know what to do, it is best to not procrastinate but to take action and get it done. *Soon but not now* often becomes *never.* When you know what you need to do, get moving and do it. Putting things off leaves them hanging around to nag us, but completing them gives us a feeling of tidy satisfaction. When there is a hill to climb, don't think that waiting will make it any smaller. If we don't put things off, we won't be pressured by having to hurry to do them at the last minute.

If there are no benefits to hurrying, then why do it? Oh, sure, sometimes we have to move a little faster to get to an appointment on time because we had something happen we didn't plan for, but that is entirely different from living in a hurry all the time. And even those times when we need to hurry to get somewhere on time probably could have been avoided had we planned better.

Living with Margin

If you have a serious hurry habit, you will probably need to locate the roots of your problem. Hurry may just be a bad habit, but it can also be the fruit of procrastination. People who procrastinate and delay—who always wait until the last minute to do things— will always be in a hurry. Learn to live with margin. That means to allocate more time to get ready to do things and get places than you think you might need. Then, if something happens that you didn't expect to happen, you will be prepared.

I am very focused and despise wasting time, so I tend to not leave much room between appointments or events, and that has often caused me to feel rushed. If anything at all goes wrong with my perfect plan, then my whole day can be off in its well-planned timing. I have learned through experiencing many frustrating days that the best plan is to leave room (margin) for the unexpected things. In other words, I have learned to expect the unexpected. If your plan for the day isn't working, make a phone call and change something if that will keep you from having to hurry. Declare war on hurry, and stay in the battle until you have detected and defeated every enemy of your peace.

Get Started Right

A few years ago I wrote a devotional called *Starting Your Day Right*, and it is one of our best-selling books. Why? Because people realize that if they can start their day right, the rest of it will go much better. If you need to break the hurry habit, say good morning to Jesus when you wake up and then declare, "I will not hurry today. I will do things today at a pace that enables me to remain peaceful, patient, and able to enjoy each task." Any time you feel yourself beginning to hurry, say it again, and again and again if that is what you have to do. This confession would be much better than saying, "I am in a hurry," about twenty times a day.

This can and should be done with any habit you are working on. If you are forming the habit of being a decisive person, then when you wake up, after greeting the Lord say, "Today I will make decisions. I am wise, I am led by the Holy Spirit, and I will not procrastinate." This is much better than saying throughout the day, "I have such a hard time making decisions."

Don't forget to practice the God habit, because the forming of all other good habits depends on it! Spend time with God and ask for His help at the beginning of the day. Doing these things will help you get your day started right.

14

Behavior 11: Emotional Habits

We all have emotions, and we never know when they will show up or go away, but we don't have to let them rule us. We can control our emotions and break up with emotional habits that harm both ourselves and others. Some emotional habits that are harmful are self-pity, depression and excessive discouragement or grief, and letting our circumstances determine our mood. Others are a quick temper, being touchy and easily offended, and taking action based on emotion without being realistic and giving thought to what we are doing. There are hundreds of emotions, but these are some of the ones we deal with most often.

Self-Pity

The habit of feeling sorry for ourselves is what I refer to as an ugly habit.

There is nothing more unattractive to look at or more unpleasant to be around than a person who is prone to self-pity. It is very draining on everyone. I know a woman who was very sweet and pleasant all of her life, and she loved doing things for other people. But at the age of eighty-seven she could no longer live alone and had to become a resident in a nursing home. The nursing home was one of the best in the city, and the staff was superior. She was taken good care of, had good meals, her children paid all the bills and visited her often, but she let the emotion of self-pity begin to rule in her life. She grumbled about and found fault with everything. She frequently said that people just didn't understand how hard it was to give up all of her stuff and have to rely on other people.

The problem became so severe that people dreaded visiting her, and the staff cringed each time she pressed the button to turn on the red flashing light outside her door, indicating that she wanted or needed something.

Thinking about the negatives in her life eventually made her angry and depressed, and sadly her doctor had to give her more and more anxiety and nerve medicine to keep her calm enough for people to handle her. I truly believe that if she had been positive and thankful, her experience could have been a joy. She was so self-absorbed that she refused to even go out of her room to visit with any of the other residents or go to the dining room, chapel, or to any function the nursing home offered. To me, this is a good example of how habitually displaying wrong emotions can literally ruin our life and relationships. She did have a choice about how she would react to this new season in her life, but she made the wrong choice and it led to miserable years for her that could have easily been avoided.

One of my greatest problems in the earlier years of my life was self-pity. It was definitely an emotion that I allowed to control me most of the time. When I didn't get what I wanted or had difficulties and problems, my first reaction was to feel sorry for myself. I had endured an abusive childhood and an unfaithful first husband and somehow I fell into the trap of thinking I had a right to feel sorry for myself. I thought that after what I had endured, it was time for me to have life easy and my way, and when that was not the case I sank into self-pity. I remember when God spoke to my heart: "Joyce, you have a reason to feel sorry for yourself, but you have no right to because I am willing and waiting to bring justice and recompense into your life." When we allow ourselves to become a victim, it threatens our future. No matter how poor a start we may have had in life, or even how bad things are now, God will always pay us back and give us double blessing for our former trouble if we are willing to do things His way. His way is not self-pity and all of the other negative emotions that go with it. I had to break the habit of self-pity, and you will need to do the same thing if it is a problem for you. Self-pity keeps you stuck with only yourself, and the self you are with isn't a happy one. You become the center of your universe. God had to show me that self-pity is actually idolatry, because when we are turned inward we are focusing on pleasing ourselves rather than focusing on God.

Self-pity is a death and has no resurrection, a sinkhole from which no recusing hand can drag you because you have chosen to sink.

Elizabeth Elliot

We cannot receive help from God or man until we make the decision to break the bad habit of sinking into self-pity when we face disappointments in life.

As with any bad habit, the way to overcome self-pity is to recognize it and realize that it is hurting you and is not pleasing to God. Then you must confess it as sin, repent, and ask for forgiveness and God's help in changing. Learn to recognize the signs that you are sinking into self-pity and say, "No, I am not going to that dark place again." Self-pity is a total waste of time, and it makes us feel lousy. It prevents God from helping us, makes us unpleasant to be with, and steals joy and peace.

If you are starting to sink into self-pity, then think about your blessings. Write them down and rehearse them out loud. Go visit or call someone who is worse off than you are. Get out and help somebody, but whatever you do, don't just sink deeper and deeper into feeling sorry for yourself. If you have a place to live, food to eat, and clothes to wear, you are better off than more than half of the world's population. If we compare ourselves to people who appear to have a better life than we do, we can easily sink into self-pity. However, if we compare ourselves to those who have less than we do, then we will feel fortunate indeed. Develop the habit of not letting emotions like self-pity control you.

Control Your Temper

> *Cease from anger, and forsake wrath;*
> *do not fret—it only causes harm.*
>
> Psalm 37:8 (NKJV)

Temper is a symptom—self is the disease. We can easily become angry and lose our peace when we don't get what we want, but we can also develop the habit of staying peaceful and not allowing our emotions to control us. Keeping "self" happy can become a full-time job, but the pay is disappointing at the end of the week. I eventually realized that the more I doted on myself, the more miserable I was. I believe that the only path to true happiness is to forget yourself and live to be a blessing to others. God will always provide our joy if we follow His guidelines for a happy life.

The Bible teaches us clearly that we are to control our temper. You may think that you can't do that, but the truth is that it is *your* temper, and only you can lose it or control it. The choice is yours. I grew up in a home where anger and turmoil were the norm. My father was an extremely angry man. He used his temper to control people through fear. I was so accustomed to anger that I didn't even know that peace was an option until I saw God's peace operating through Dave.

Righteous or Unrighteous Anger?

Righteous anger is a divine emotion, but it is anger directed toward evil rather than all the people and things in our life that inconvenience us. If we are going to get angry, why not get angry enough at poverty to do something about it? Or so angry at human trafficking that you pray and participate in some way in rescuing those enslaved by this terrible tragedy? Recently one of our medical teams was in an area of the world where sex trafficking is rampant, and due to the extreme poverty that exists there, many parents sell off one or two of their children for five hundred dollars in order to prevent the other five or six from starving. They rationalize that at least the ones they sell will be fed, and the price they get for them will feed the ones who are left behind. They have no true understanding that they are selling their children into a life of torment, disease, and slavery. Thankfully, we are negotiating right now with traffickers in that area to buy the girls back—girls who were already in a container waiting to be shipped to another country where they would be forced into prostitution. It will cost three thousand dollars but is worth every penny to save them from the life they would be facing. We are angry about this evil in the world today, but it is a righteous anger that moves us to action. I wasted too much of my life in unrighteous anger, being angry because I wasn't getting everything I wanted, and I refuse to waste any more of it. Are you at that point yet? I hope you are, and that you will start being in control of your anger instead of allowing it to control you.

While there is righteous anger, that usually isn't the kind of anger we experience. Moreover, that isn't what gets us into trouble. The type of anger that we usually feel is unrighteous anger. It is the anger that triggers pain and damage not only to others but also to ourselves.

The emotion of unrighteous anger is a disease waiting to happen. Frequent anger places undue stress on us and is the root cause of many illnesses. Doctors from Coral Gables, Florida, compared the efficiency of the heart's pumping action in eighteen men with coronary artery disease to nine healthy controls. Each of the study participants underwent one physical stress test (riding an exercise bicycle) and three mental stress tests (doing math problems in their heads, recalling a recent incident that had made them very angry, and giving a short speech to defend themselves against a hypothetical charge of shoplifting). Using sophisticated X-ray techniques, the doctors took pictures of the subjects' hearts in action during these tests.

For all the subjects, anger reduced the amount of blood that the heart pumped to body tissues more than the other tests did, and this was especially true for those who had heart disease.

The doctors administering the tests commented, "Why anger is so much more potent than fear or mental stress is anybody's guess. But until we see more research on this subject, it couldn't hurt to count to ten before you blow your stack."

God's interpretation of "Don't blow your stack" is "Hold your peace" (Exodus 14:14). He has given us His peace, but we have to hold on to it when the temptation to lose it arrives at our doorstep. I know that it is possible to break the habit of letting the emotion of unrighteous anger control us and to enjoy the peace of God at all times.

Emotional Reactions

We have learned behaviors that cause us to react to a variety of situations without even thinking. They are habits that have been formed through years of repetition. When we are upset, we react one way; when we are discouraged, it may be another way. When we are hurt, we may react in a completely different way than when we are upset or discouraged. Jesus experienced all of these emotions and yet He always reacted the same way. He trusted God and remained peaceful. Can we do the same thing? Yes, we can! Begin paying attention to how you react in situations and record your observations in a journal. Before long you will realize that you are reacting to emotional stimuli instead of purposely acting according to God's instructions in His Word. You can develop a new habit of remaining stable in all circumstances.

If I feel sorry for myself and angry when someone hurts my feelings, then I am reacting to the emotions they stirred up in me. That puts them in control of my life, and that is not a good thing. However, if I forgive them, which is what Jesus teaches us to do, then God is controlling my life, and that is a wonderful thing. If we allow what other people do to us and other circumstances to control our behavior, then we become a slave to our emotions. On the other hand, if we are willingly led by the Word of God and by His Spirit, we become Servants of God and can expect to enjoy life and all God has promised us.

Emotional Wounds

Everyone experiences emotional wounds in their life, some of them deeper than others. We all must learn not to allow our emotions to control us, but people who have been deeply wounded emotionally may have more difficulty doing so than others. If a person has been rejected, abandoned, or abused, it is probable that their emotions do not function as they would if they had been spared those traumas. If love and acceptance have been withheld or you have been made to feel that you have no value, you fit into the category of people God calls the brokenhearted. But I have good news for you. Jesus came to heal the broken-hearted, to give them beauty for ashes, joy for mourning, and praise for heaviness. He also came to exchange turmoil for peace.

I have been the recipient of God's healing in my life and I hope you have also. However, if you are in need of this kind of heal-ing, I want to assure you that Jesus is waiting with open arms to begin a miraculous restoration in your life. If your emotions are wounded, you may have emotional habits that are harmful to you.

Do you eat for comfort when you are hurt or upset? Many peo-ple who have a habit of overeating run to the refrigerator for com-fort when they should be going to God.

Do you go shopping and spend money that you don't have when you're hurting? If so, you are trying to buy comfort. What-ever comfort we obtain from pampering our flesh is temporary at best, but the deep wound that needs God's healing touch is still in us. Whether it is eating, shopping, gambling, drugs, alcohol, or any other destructive behavior, God can and will deliver peo-ple with those problems. He is the God of all healing and com-fort. He is our Deliverer! The first step to freedom is to recognize the truth about why we do what we do and be determined that, with God's help, we will not stay in bondage.

People do all sorts of things when they are upset or feel emo-tionally down in any way. These emotions cause stress, and peo-ple revert to habits—things that we do often without even being aware that we are doing them—for relief. Learn to run to God in times of stress instead of to the habit or addiction you normally turn to. Jesus simply says, "Come unto Me."

Habit or Addiction?

When is a destructive behavior a habit and when is it an addiction? We can have varying degrees of habits that more or less have control over us. But when a destructive habit is taken to extremes, then it usually becomes an addiction, something that one must do in order to feel calm or satisfied.

When I smoked cigarettes I automatically reached for a cigarette many times a day, but especially when I was in a stressful situation. I was addicted to the nicotine and had to go through a period of discomfort physically, emotionally, and mentally in order to stop smoking. I never said, "I am addicted to cigarettes." I said, "I have a bad habit of smoking cigarettes." I believe we feel more comfortable thinking that we have a bad habit rather than that we are addicted to anything. Did I have a bad habit or was I addicted? I am not exactly sure when a habit becomes an addiction, but I think the answer is the same. The process of healing may be more difficult if a habit has become an addiction, but it is self-defeating to think that if we are addicted to something, we are stuck with the problem and just cannot help doing what we do.

Addicts may feel that they have no choice in their behavior. They think they are addicted and must do what they do. When we see something as a habit, we are more inclined to believe the bad habit can be broken. But I assure you that whatever category your problem falls into—you can be set completely free.

Whether the problem is biting your fingernails or a heroin addiction, the answer is still the same: God will help you! I don't mean that to sound overly simplified, but in reality it is. He is our Helper! Will breaking these habits or addictions be easy? No! Is it possible? Yes, absolutely yes! If you are addicted to any kind of behavior that is destructive, you are hurting and suffering and may feel trapped and hopeless, but God offers us hope in Him. You will go through suffering while you are giving up these habits and addictions, but it will be a suffering that will eventually bring joy.

When you are suffering the symptoms that go along with change of any kind, always remember: THE SUFFERING WILL COME TO AN END!

CHAPTER

15

Behavior 12: The Confidence Habit

Success comes in cans, not can'ts.

Anonymous

Can confidence become a habit, or is it something that we must wait to feel? I firmly believe we can become habitually confident. What is confidence? It is the belief that you are capable and able to do whatever it is that needs to be done. The world calls it self-confidence, but God's Word calls it *confidence in Christ*. If my confidence is in me, I am likely to be regularly disappointed in my ability to perform or remain stable, but if my confidence is firmly planted in Christ, I can be assured that He will always remain the same.

I have strength for all things in Christ Who empowers me
[I am ready for anything and equal to anything through Him

Who infuses inner strength into me; I am self-sufficient in Christ's sufficiency].

Philippians 4:13

This is a Scripture verse that I turn to frequently to remind myself that through Christ, I can do whatever I need to do in life. I think we do need to be reminded because there are lots of people ready and waiting to tell us what we can't do and what we are not. Sally Field said, "It took me a long time not to judge myself through someone else's eyes." Let's stop giving others consent to make us feel inferior, and let's believe what God says about us in His Word.

What does He say? Here are five things He says that will encourage you.

1. You are loved perfectly and completely (I John 4:16–18).
2. You are accepted and will never be rejected by Him if you believe (John 3:18).
3. You have talents and abilities (Romans 12:6).
4. God created you uniquely and you should not compare yourself with others (Psalm 139:13–16).
5. You can do whatever you need to do through Christ and not be afraid of failing (Philippians 4:13).

I chose these five things because they have all ministered to me greatly in my own life. I was insecure and lacked true confidence for the first forty years of my life, but believing God's Word has given me confidence and a new life. It will do the same thing for you.

Merely reading the Scriptures above did not initially change me. I had to learn to think them over and over in my mind and speak them out of my mouth. I have looked at them hundreds if not thousands of times and let them soak into my consciousness. They have renewed my mind and changed me and my attitude about myself and my relationship with God. I now have the confidence habit, and you can have it too. We can either believe what God says, or we can believe what we think and what people say. I think God is the best and most reliable choice.

Inside Out

Being confident will ultimately enable us to live a bolder life and do things we would not do without confidence, but the most important things that it does for us lie inside of us. Our true life is in us, and it is not found in what we own or what we do for a living or who we know or how highly educated we are. These things may be part of a confident person's life, but they are not the most important part of anyone's life. Some people mistakenly think they are, and they waste their life striving to improve their outer life without ever paying attention to their inner life.

A confident person is at rest in her soul. Jesus promised us that if we would come to Him, He would give us rest, ease, refreshment, recreation, and blessed quiet for our souls (Matthew 11:29). Doesn't that sound absolutely wonderful? Rest for our souls is vital. We can lay our body down and get physical rest but not be truly resting because our soul (mind, will, emotions) is still working the entire time. Give your soul a vacation!

Being at rest internally is worth more than anything we own or will ever do. There are many seemingly confident and successful people who are miserable inside. I think it is important for each of us to realize what is most important and have a goal to obtain it. Have you paid more attention to your outer life than to your inner? If so, this is a good time to make a change.

God's Word teaches us to put no confidence in what we are in the flesh, on outward privileges and advantages, but instead to find our confidence in Christ alone (Philippians 3:3). If we do that, we will have a blessed quiet for our souls that nothing else compares to. The confidence of knowing that God loves, accepts, and approves of you is the best thing you can ever have.

God Is with You

Do you have the confidence that God is with you at all times? He is, and He wants all of us to have that assurance. Not just a mere hope, but assurance! Even when we don't feel His presence or see any evidence that He is with us, we can have complete confidence that He is. He has promised to never leave us or forsake us but to be with us always. You are never alone. God is omnipresent, and that means that He is everywhere, all the time.

Where could I go from Your Spirit? Or where could I flee from Your presence?

If I ascend up into heaven, You are there; if I make
my bed in Sheol (the place of the dead), behold,
You are there.
If I take the wings of the morning or dwell in the
uttermost parts of the sea,
even there shall Your hand lead me, and
Your right hand shall hold me.

Psalm 139:7–10

We can see from this Psalm written by David that he enjoyed the kind of confidence I am speaking about, and we can and should enjoy it also. You and I can confidently face any situation or challenge or any new thing that might try to intimidate or frighten us. As we approach it we can say to ourselves, "Through Christ's strength and by placing my confidence in Him, I can do this!"

Make a Decision

I urge you to make a decision that you will not be a timid, insecure, doubtful person, but that you will be confident. When I am ministering to crowds of people, I have to just decide to be confident no matter how I might feel. I cannot always discern from watching people if they approve of me or of what I am saying, or even how interested they are. We cannot look to others to make us feel confident, because if we do, then we will always need a fresh fix of approving nods, glances, and words of acceptance in order to be stable.

I went through a lot of agony trying to minister to people for a long time. If anyone got up and left the conference when I was teaching, I felt sure that they didn't like me or what I was saying. If anyone looked bored or sleepy, I immediately thought that I was the problem. I let their faces dictate my level of confidence, and I had to stop it or be miserable the rest of my life. Do you want to spend your life looking for approval, or have the assurance that you have God's approval and that is all you truly need?

Confidence is not a feeling we have; it is a right mind-set. We can think that people don't like us or that they do, so why do most people lean toward the negative? They lean that way because the devil is influencing their thinking, and they either are not aware of it or they don't take aggressive action to reclaim their thoughts. We can be afraid that we are going to fail, or we can expect to succeed.

Be Aggressive in Your Approach to Life

True godly aggression begins in the inner man. Be bold and aggressive, approaching each day with confidence, expecting to be successful in whatever you do that day. If we have a quiet, confident inner attitude, we will never have any problem doing what we need to do. Confidence is not a feeling that we must work up and then go out into the world and move fast, talk loud, and often be obnoxious. It is a quiet and beautiful thing that begins in the heart and stands firm in its conviction that we are not alone and we are able. The attitude of the confident person is filled with cans, not can'ts. It is firm, steadfast, and strong in the Lord.

Approach every area of life with confidence. If you are facing a major change at this time in your life, don't be afraid of it. You can be confident that it will be a new season of blessing. If you are in the midst of some trial or difficulty, even in that you can be confident that God has a plan and that He will never allow more to happen to you than you can bear. He will provide a way out, and you will gain valuable experience that will aid you in the future.

Prayer and Confidence

Prayer is a major part of our life as children of God, and we must pray with confidence that God hears and wants to meet our needs and right desires. God doesn't want us to approach Him timidly, fearfully, and without confidence. He instructs us to come boldly to His throne to ask for what we need and want. We are never told to sneak up to the throne or to crawl as a beggar. We know Jesus, and we have the use of His wonderful and powerful name so we can and should go boldly.

Consider these two verses of Scripture:

And I will do [I Myself will grant] whatever you ask in My Name [as presenting all that I AM], so that the Father may be glorified and extolled in (through) the Son.

[Yes] I will grant [I Myself will do for you] whatever you shall ask in My Name [as presenting all that I AM].

John 14:13–14

Not only is what Jesus says amazing, but He says it two times in a row. To me, that means He really wants us to get it. Asking for "whatever" doesn't sound timid or fearful to me. It sounds like confidence that we are loved and can come boldly to God knowing that we are loved and He wants to meet our needs. God wants to be involved in everything we do, and we invite Him into our business through prayer.

Here is a truly amazing Scripture:

You who [are His servants and by your prayers] put the Lord in remembrance [of His promises], keep not silence.

Isaiah 62:6b

It requires confidence to actually remind God what He has promised you. Imagine a child coming to his father and saying, "Dad, you promised that you would play ball with me tonight." That is a beautiful example of a child who is confident in his dad's love. But it was a bit more difficult for me to believe I could go to Father God in that same way, reminding Him of His promises to me. Over the years I have gained enough confidence to do that, and I see amazing results. Yesterday as I prayed I said something like this: "Father, You have promised to give me favor so I am expecting to see it today. You have promised to give me strength to do all things, so I am expecting to be energized by Your strength for all of my tasks today. You are my wisdom, so I expect that I will not do anything foolish today. I will make wise decisions." On and on I went, reminding God of His promises, and I bore witness in my spirit that it was right to do it. I have decided to have this kind of confidence by faith. I do it because I believe God wants me to and because it is important to the fulfillment of His plan, and you can do it too.

Now here is another even more amazing Scripture:

Put Me in remembrance [remind Me of your merits]; let us plead *and* argue together. Set forth your case, that you may be justified (proved right).

Isaiah 43:26

Being "in Christ" is the one true merit that we need, based on the New Covenant. God will bless us because we believe in His Son, Jesus. True confidence presses in and won't let go of God. Jacob wrestled with the angel of the Lord all night and refused to let him go until God blessed him.

And Jacob was left alone, and a Man wrestled with him until daybreak.

And when [the Man] saw that He did not prevail against [Jacob], He touched the hollow of his thigh; and Jacob's thigh was put out of joint as he wrestled with Him.

Then He said, Let Me go, for day is breaking. But [Jacob] said, I will not let You go unless You declare a blessing upon me.

Genesis 32:24–26

Jacob had been a cheat, a liar, and a swindler, but he wanted to make things right with God and his brother Esau whose birthright he had stolen. He obviously had the confidence in God to wrestle with Him until he received a blessing. This is shocking to those of us who have had difficulty being bold in prayer or in our approach to God. But here it is in black-and-white, written in God's Word. Jacob's confidence and boldness won him power with God. I guess God liked his confident attitude!

There are other examples of this in the Bible. There is the parable of the widow who went to the unjust judge and kept pestering him until he vindicated her. She wore down an unjust judge (Luke 18:1–8). How much more will our just God do for those who press and won't give up? Jesus began this parable by saying that His disciples "ought always to pray and not to turn coward (faint, lose heart, and give up)." He wanted them to press with confidence, and He wants us to do the same thing. Remember, our confidence isn't in ourselves, it is in Christ. We should always keep in mind that without Him, we are nothing and can do nothing that merits anything, but through Him we have a right to go to God boldly in Jesus' Name.

Without confidence we are like jet airliners with no fuel. We just sit and do nothing. But with confidence we can go places and take people with us. We can enjoy our journey in life because at all times we have blessed rest and quiet for our souls.

Study confidence until you are firmly fixed in faith that God does indeed want you to live with it. Refuse to do without it. Make it a habit!

CHAPTER
16

Behavior 13: The Habit of Adding Value to Others

Pretend that every single person you meet has a
sign around his or her neck that says, Make Me Feel
Important. Not only will you succeed in sales, you
will succeed in life.

Mary Kay Ash

Every one of us needs encouragement on a regular basis. I believe
one of the greatest things we can do in life is to form the habit
of adding value to everyone we come in contact with. Remember that a habit is formed through repetition; therefore, focusing
on doing this every day is the key to success. If adding value to
everyone that you meet is the habit you want to develop, be creative in finding methods that will remind you to do so.

If you need reminders, write yourself a note that you will have
to read, or make a sign and put it the first place you will be after

getting out of bed. After seeing your reminder I suggest you even say to yourself or out loud, "Today I will add value to everyone I meet." Even if encouraging others does not come easily to you, you can develop the habit of doing it. I know, because I have done that in my own life.

Focusing on adding value to other people will help us take our minds off ourselves, and that is a very good thing. Being self-centered is the root cause of most of the world's misery, and anything we do to avoid it in our lives is a plus. People with my type of personality, commonly called type A or choleric, are very focused individuals, but they usually focus on what they are trying to accomplish. As a result of that focus, they can often be guilty of being insensitive to the needs and desires of other people. All personality types have strengths and weaknesses. The type A or choleric person's tendency to be insensitive to other people is a weakness, and it must be confronted and overcome with God's help. We should never use people to get what we want, and if they help us get what we want or reach our goal, we should give them credit and value them all the more. This is something that God has helped me overcome and it has made me a better leader and person. I am sure I still make mistakes, but I have made lots of progress over the years. If this is a weakness for you, admit it, and start right now overcoming it with God's help. You and He together can do anything!

There are people who are gifted by God with a special ability to encourage others. The Bible says in Romans 12:8, when speaking about giving ourselves to exercising the gifts that we have, "**(He who exhorts (encourages), to his exhortation; he who contrib-**

utes, let him do it in simplicity *and* liberality; he who gives aid *and* superintends, with zeal *and* singleness of mind; he who does acts of mercy, with genuine cheerfulness *and* joyful eagerness." Even if you feel that encouraging others is not a particular gift for you, you are still responsible to do it. God's Word teaches us that we are to encourage one another.

The people who are gifted to encourage others will find that it comes very naturally to them. It won't be a habit they will have to develop, but thankfully it can become one for the rest of us.

God is the Source "of every comfort (consolation and encouragement)" (2 Corinthians 1:3). Since God is an encourager, we should be the same way, because He is our example in all things. Any time we do what God does we can be assured that we are doing the things that are right and that will produce joy, peace, and power for our own lives. The more you encourage others, the better you will feel and the more joy you will have. We reap what we sow; therefore, if we sow joy we will reap joy. If we sow encouragement, we can expect encouragement from others. When we encourage others it builds them up and makes them strong. They are enabled to press forward; however, without that encouragement they might become weary and give up.

You have it easily in your power to increase the sum total of this world's happiness now. How? By giving a few words of sincere appreciation to someone who is lonely or discouraged. Perhaps you will forget tomorrow the kind words you say today, but the recipient may cherish them over a lifetime.

Dale Carnegie

We have been entrusted with a great power. We have the power to encourage and to add value to everyone we meet. What a wonderful goal to start each day with!

There are many ways we can encourage other people. We can do it with words, through contributing to help pay for something they may need, and through giving aid to them in some way. We can also encourage people by being quick to forgive, to cover offenses (1 Peter 4:8), withhold criticism, and bear with and be patient with their weaknesses (Galatians 6:2). I sure appreciate it when people don't make a big deal out of my mistakes. It is wonderfully refreshing when we make a mistake and the person who was affected by it says, "Don't worry about it, it is not a problem. We all make mistakes."

Another way to add value is to listen with interest to what people say. None of us like it when we are trying to talk to someone and it is obvious they are not interested in what we are saying. It makes us feel devalued. There are, of course, some people who rattle on and on, and listening to them for as long as they want to talk may not be possible, but at least we can exit the conversation respectfully.

We can encourage and add value to people through extending mercy to them. God's Word says that mercy is greater than judgment. People who notice everything anyone does that is wrong are referred to as faultfinders. They seem to usually notice what is wrong and they always mention it, but they seldom see what is right. Even when they do see what is right, their critical nature prevents them from talking about it. Instead of showing mercy and not mentioning the fault or mistake, they rehearse it over and over, not only to the person with the fault but to other people also. They find it hard to drop it and let it go, which is part of the definition of forgiveness. I know how people like that affect me, and I sure don't want to be one of them. Do you? Jesus had the habit of being merciful, kind, and forgiving, and I want it, too, don't you?

We should make a big deal out of anything good that anyone does and learn to cover their faults with mercy. Let's make them feel better when they make mistakes instead of making them feel worse.

God Cares About How We Treat People

I was in a jewelry store the other day and a young man was polishing the counter and paying no attention to me. I wanted to see something in the case, and even when I asked him if he could help me, he didn't answer. I felt irritated and asked him again, but my tone of voice could have been nicer than it was. He finally looked up and when he did, I could tell that he was a little mentally impaired, and he said, "I can't open the case, but I will get someone who can." Because he had his face down while polishing the glass, which was probably the job he had been hired to do, I could not see his condition. Naturally, I felt absolutely terrible about my impatient and irritated attitude and repented immediately. I still felt grieved by my attitude even an hour later. He may not have even noticed it, but God certainly let me know that He noticed it and didn't like it. Ouch!

God cares about how we treat all people, and especially people who are disadvantaged in any way. As a matter of fact, I truly believe that how we treat the people in our life is very important to God. He loves people and wants us to love them as part of our service to Him. I have often said that the measure of our love can be seen in how we treat people. Perhaps one of the greatest and most beautiful habits we can develop is the habit of being gentle, patient, loving, and adding value to each person we meet. People may forget what you said and what you did, but they will never forget how you made them feel. Make each individual feel as if they matter and are valuable.

Here is something that happened that I am sure put a smile on God's face. The story is entitled "You Are Going Places," and the author is unknown.

It was another dreary and gloomy day. I had come home from school, changed my clothes and gotten ready for work. I work at a local restaurant in town as a cashier, seater, and busser. I went to work feeling down and out. And to make matters worse I was busing that evening. It's the same thing over and over again. Dealing with customers who complain and whine about their food, where they sat and how the piece of pie that they are served is too big or too small. Little things like that tend to annoy a lot of our employees but we all learn to deal with it. Some days it is annoying but you just get used to it I guess. I know I have.

Three elderly ladies walked in and were sat at a booth by the windows. It happened to be the very spot near where I bus and keep the dirty dishes in the bins. I had been busing since 5:00 p.m. and we were quite busy. Trying to keep up with all the dirty tables, people leaving and coming in and servers running all over the restaurant, it was crazy.

But these elderly women were watching how I was busing and working really hard to make sure every table was clean and ready for the next customers. When they were finished with their meals, I took their plates back to the kitchen. They talked to me for a while about school, how I was doing, what grade I was in, and what I planned to do in the future.

As they were leaving, they walked past me, and one of them said to me in a confident and gentle voice, "You are going places." And that was it. They left the restaurant and I was pretty much in awe. **I had tears in my eyes, because they gave me a reason to believe in myself.** *They picked my spirit up from being down and out and gave me a reason to keep on working hard and to give it my all.*

People told me that I couldn't have a career in television until I had a degree and was out of college. I'm now an executive producer and co-anchor of a student-produced television show. I just finished an internship at a local television station this past summer. And the best thing is, I'm only 17 years old and I am a senior in high school.

Reading this story brought conviction of a bad attitude to me because Dave talks to waiters and waitresses in this same way all the time, and I am often trying to get him to stop so we can order our food or get our bill. I assumed he was pestering them until I read this story, so reading it taught me a lesson. Now I will have to wait patiently while Dave encourages them and perhaps changes their life. Just two days ago he took time to talk with the waitress and the person busing the table. In between him talking to the two of them, while no one was at the table but us, I said, "Will you stop asking these people so many questions so we can order our food and go?" He said, "No, I believe it encourages people when we care about them and their life." I guess I wanted him to encourage people without taking so long to do it. Well, another lesson learned the hard way for Miss Joyce!

There are persons who seem to overcome obstacles and by character and perseverance to have risen to the top. But we have no record of the number of able persons who fall by the wayside, persons who, with enough encouragement and opportunity, might make great contributions.

Mary Barnett Gilson

Considering this statement does make me wonder how many people were intended for great things, but the people who were assigned the job by God of encouraging them didn't think their part was important enough to bother doing it. We should try to see the potential in people instead of the problems. I had plenty of problems, but thankfully Dave saw the potential and he has been a huge encouragement to me in many ways. Most of us need someone to encourage us as we make our journey in life.

The world needs encouragers, but sadly not enough people see it as important, so they don't bother doing it. Adding value to everyone you meet may be one of the most important things you do in life. It may help many succeed who might have otherwise failed in their pursuits. Most people don't place enough value on seemingly little things like encouragement, but I don't believe it is a little thing to God.

Become a person who habitually encourages others, and you will find that doing so adds joy to your own life.

Cheering Others On

We should be able to be happy for people when they succeed. Even if they are about to surpass us, we should cheer them on.

Forty thousand fans were on hand in the Oakland stadium when Rickey Henderson tied Lou Brock's career stolen-base record. According to *USA Today*, Lou Brock, who had left baseball in 1979, had followed Henderson's career and was excited about his success. Realizing that Rickey would set a new record, Brock said, "I'll be there. Do you think I'm going to miss it now? Rickey did in 12 years what took me 19. He's amazing."

The real success stories in life are with people who can rejoice in the successes of others. What Lou Brock did in cheering on Rickey Henderson should be a way of life for those in the family of God. Few circumstances give us a better opportunity to exhibit God's grace than when someone succeeds and surpasses us in an area of our own strength and reputation.

I can only imagine how good it made Rickey Henderson feel to have Lou Brock at the game cheering him on. We all want our peers to be happy for us when we succeed. Let's remember that we don't have to be in competition for the number one spot in life in all things, and that no matter how good we are at something, someone is on the way who will be better at what we do than we are. That is progress, and we should be thankful for it. They say records were made to be broken, and I am glad they are because that way we can all keep trying to do better and cheering for whoever succeeds.

CHAPTER
17

Behavior 14: The Habit of Discipline

He who lives without discipline dies
without honor.
Icelandic proverb

By now, you've probably realized that none of these habits can be developed without a lot of discipline and self-control. Just wanting to do better is not enough; we have to be willing to discipline ourselves, and that always means giving something up in order to get something we want more. We discipline ourselves now for a future reward.

For the time being no discipline brings joy, but seems griev-ous *and* painful; but afterwards it yields a peaceable fruit of righteousness to those who have been trained by it [a har-vest of fruit which consists in righteousness—in conformity to God's will in purpose, thought, and action, resulting in right living and right standing with God].

Hebrews 12:11

We often hear people say, "I'm not a very disciplined person," or "I wish I were a more disciplined person." Discipline never comes by wishing, but it comes only by a willingness to go through what is grievous and painful in order to get to the good thing on the other side of it. Are you willing? I guess you should stop right here for a few minutes and make that decision before going on. If you make the decision and you are serious about it, you can depend on God to give you the strength to follow through, but I am not going to try to deceive you by saying that forming all of these new habits will be easy. I would rather underpromise and overdeliver than overpromise and underdeliver. If it turns out not to be difficult or painful, that's great, but if it does turn out to be difficult or painful, I don't want you to run because you had no idea what you were getting into.

Some of the habits you need to break or make will be easier than others, but there will surely be some that will require great discipline and self-control. Don't be afraid of pain, but remember the old adage, "No pain, no gain." Any time something is hard, say to yourself, "I am making progress."

Never Quit

Most things in life don't come easily and quickly. And certainly most things that are worth having don't come that way. We have all heard of Albert Einstein. He is known for his brilliant mind, but he said, **"It's not that I'm so smart, it's just that I stay with problems longer."**

I think one of my better traits has been that I don't give up easily. It is amazing what you can accomplish if you are willing to go through the hard part to get to the good part. Perseverance and steadfastness are wonderful qualities to have and ones that every successful person does have.

> Perseverance is a great element of success. If you knock long enough and loud enough at the gate, you are sure to wake up somebody.
>
> *Henry Wadsworth Longfellow*

Always remember that nobody can make you give up if you refuse to, and nobody can keep you from succeeding if you won't give up. My point is that your success in life or any venture is between you and God. As long as what you are attempting to do is in His will for you, He will help you do it, if you will do your part. I have said many times, "We are partners with God in life. He will always do His part, but are we willing to do our part?" I pray that we always are.

Some of the habits you will be working on will come more easily than others, and I don't know that I have a good answer as to why. During the years I have been working out at the gym with a strength coach, she often tries to help me learn things that will enhance the benefit of the exercise I am doing, things like standing certain ways, or not slouching my shoulders while I am doing certain exercises, or not dropping my head but keeping it erect.

Some of them become a habit after she reminds me only two or three times, and some of them I still need to be reminded of after six years. But I have already decided that I am not giving up no matter how long it takes me to get it right.

One of the hardest things for me to remember when I am doing my exercises has been to not do them too fast. I think most of us want to get it over with, and my personality is a conquer-and-move-on personality anyway, so between these two things I have needed a lot of reminders to slow down so the muscle I am using gets the intended benefit. Well, the good news is that at this point when I hear my coach say, "Slow down," I already know she is going to say it. I am finally recognizing it myself when I do things too fast, so that means I am very close to overcoming in that area. Yeah!

Habits are things that we often do unconsciously, and to break bad ones we have to become conscious and aware that we are doing them and then move on to being aware before we do it so we can choose not to do it. It is a process, and if you are a person who gives up easily, you won't get very far. So make a decision right now that you are in for the long haul and that you are willing to have the pain for the gain.

You might be wishing that you could have a coach for all areas of life to remind you when you are doing the wrong thing so that you can do the right thing. If that is true, then I have good news for you. You can count on your life coach, the Holy Spirit, to always remind you when you are getting lax in one of your good habits and beginning to revert to old ones. He brings things to our remembrance (John 14:26).

Life coaches have become popular today. They are people who help clients learn how to live their lives in the best way possible, and their training covers many areas of life. I am sure they are a blessing to lots of people, and if you want to pay one you can, but you already have the best one that has ever been available, and that is the Holy Spirit. He teaches us all things. Jesus said,

> But the Comforter (Counselor, Helper, Intercessor, Advocate, Strengthener, Standby), the Holy Spirit, Whom the Father will send in My name [in My place, to represent Me and act on My behalf], He will teach you all things. And He will cause you to recall (will remind you of, bring to your remembrance) everything I have told you.
>
> *John 14:26*

Isn't that wonderful news! We don't have to try to do it alone. We have a Divine Helper Who will not only remind us what to do but will strengthen us to be able to do it. Lean on Him at all times! I can promise you that if you will not give up, He certainly won't give up on you.

When you're weary and tempted to give up, just remember that your breakthrough may only be one day away.

As you begin your journey of developing better habits and breaking bad ones, you might want to start with a couple that might be a little easier for you to have some quick victories under your belt before tackling some of the harder ones. Don't keep putting the harder ones off too long, however, or you just might never get around to them. The ones that are the most difficult are probably the ones that will be the most beneficial to you when you have had victory. If a door is difficult to open, don't walk away, just push a little harder.

Discipline and Joy

Although discipline doesn't bring joy immediately, it is intended to bring joy ultimately. God wants us to be happy. He wants us to enjoy our lives, and I personally don't think that we ever will unless we are committed to a life of discipline and self-control. People who cannot control themselves are not happy people. They feel bad about themselves, they are pressured by feelings of guilt and failure, and they often take their anger and frustration out on other people. Surely it would be far better to go through the pain of learning discipline than to remain in a state of permanent slavery and misery to sin and destructive habits.

Jesus came that we might have and enjoy life abundantly and fully (John 10:10). Are you doing that? If not, is it due to a habit you have that needs to be broken? If the answer is yes, then get started. Remember, the experts say it takes twenty-one to thirty days to make or break a habit, so every day you keep going and refuse to give up brings you one day closer to freedom.

Don't think about the difficulty of forming new habits, but instead think about the joy and freedom that is soon to come. I also recommend that you not count how many days you have left to go before the new habit kicks in. It is best rather to think in terms of how many days you have practiced doing the thing that you want to become part of your habitual behavior. For example, if disciplining yourself to eat healthy snacks instead of sugary ones is your goal, then think and talk about how far you have come each day that you are successful rather than how hard it is for you to do without sugar. Verbalizing how difficult it is for you twenty times a day will only make it more difficult, but verbalizing your joy in having been successful one day, two days, three days, and so on will make you happy. As I have said, what we think becomes our reality, so be sure your thoughts line up with your ultimate desires.

The Safety Zone

We can live safely or dangerously, but if we want to live safely, or in what I like to call the Safety Zone, then discipline and self-control are required. For example, if I want to be safe from the burden of debt, I must discipline myself regularly not to spend more money than I have. The ease in obtaining credit cards today allows people to overspend by permitting them to spend tomorrow's income today. If we do that, however, when tomorrow comes we have already spent our money and we have to keep borrowing. It is an endless cycle unless we learn to never buy something we cannot pay for with comfort. If you want to use credit cards for convenience, that is fine, but pay them off at the end of each month. If you are not able to do that right now, then make it your goal and start working toward it.

Some people are so accustomed to living on borrowed money that even the thought of what I am saying sounds like an impossibility, but I can assure you that it is not only possible, it is the only safe way to live. You may already be deep in debt, but don't think that it is too late for you to do anything about it. Today's discipline will help you overcome past mistakes if you keep at it long enough.

Are you living an unsustainable life? Some of you may even say from time to time, "I can't keep this up forever," when it comes to the stress level in your life, the debt that keeps mounting higher and higher, the weight you may be gaining, or any other area that has become habitually out of control. If you know that you cannot keep up the behavior, then why put off stopping it? It won't be any easier if you wait longer, and it could possibly be more difficult.

Just this morning the Holy Spirit convicted me of an area in my life that needs more discipline. I have learned over the years that when God brings conviction He also gives grace to conquer. Timing is important! It is important that we act in His timing, not in ours. Putting something off until a more convenient time usually means that we either never do it or we do it with great struggle. I started today praying about the area I was convicted in and studying the best way to make changes. "Act right away, don't delay!"

Life with Limits

The phrase "Take the Limits Off" is popular today, but is it biblical? We don't want to limit what God can do in our life through unbelief, but if we ignore healthy and wise limits, we are asking for disaster. Even good things can become bad things if we impose no limits. For example, if you spend so much time being good to other people that you have no time to take care of yourself properly, your good intention will eventually cause you health and perhaps emotional problems. Boundaries, borders, or limits are vital in every area of life. Establishing and keeping them requires discipline and the forming of good habits. I think it would be safe to say that discipline and good habits go hand in hand, just as no discipline and bad habits do.

Some people cringe at the mention of the word *discipline*. They have a mental attitude toward it that is unhealthy and self-defeating. We need to see that discipline is our friend, not our enemy. It helps us be what we say we want to be, do what we say we want to do, and have what we say we want to have. Saying what one wants is easy and costs nothing, but obtaining it requires discipline. Discipline doesn't prevent us from having fun and doing what we want to in life, but instead it helps us obtain what we truly want, which is peace, joy, and right relationships as well as other things.

We should love discipline and embrace it as our companion in life. We should invite it to be with us at all times, because it is always ready to keep us out of trouble. God's Word teaches us that only a fool hates discipline.

Most of the people I have encountered whose lives are like a train wreck are not disciplined individuals. They live by emotion rather than principle, and wisdom is far from them. They eventually have nothing left but regret in their life over what they have or have not done. We can all have the pain of discipline or the pain of regret. Wise people will discipline themselves, and that means that they do today what they will be happy with later on in life.

Expectation

You can look forward to the future expectantly if you are ready to put the principles in this book to work in your life. Every day can be an adventure in improvement rather than another day wasted. Every good habit you form will make your life better, and it will increase your joy.

I have found in my own life that if I don't take any action to move forward, I always slide backward. We don't remain stagnant for long. God is on the move and so is Satan, and we must decide which one we are going to move with. God's plan for your life is amazingly wonderful, but Satan comes only to kill, steal, and destroy (John 10:10). Reading this book won't help you at all unless you make some decisions and follow through, so I pray you are ready to do that. If you are, then I can promise you that you and God together are an unbeatable team.

SUMMARY

When you want to make or break a habit, do the following:

- Choose one area and begin.
- Don't feel overwhelmed by all the changes that are needed. One thing at a time, one day at a time is the best plan.
- Be clear about what you want to accomplish.
- Pray and secure God's help.
- Focus on doing the right thing, instead of not doing the wrong thing. (We overcome evil with good.)
- Don't expect instant results. Be prepared to be committed for twenty-one to thirty days, and longer if necessary.
- Develop a support system to help you remember the new habit you are developing:
    1. Put up signs where you will see them often.
    2. Depend on the Holy Spirit to remind you when you get off track.
    3. Ask a friend or family member to remind you if you're reverting to old ways.
- Line up your thoughts and words with what you want to see happen.
- Celebrate every day of success.

- When you make mistakes, shake off the disappointment and keep going forward.
- Don't be discouraged by how far you have to go.
- Never give up!

> *Watch your thoughts, for they become words.*
> *Watch your words, for they become actions.*
> *Watch your actions, for they become habits.*
> *Watch your habits, for they become character.*
> *Watch your character, for it becomes your destiny.*
>
> —*Anonymous*

Do you wish this wasn't the end?
Are you hungry for more great teaching, inspiring
testimonies, ideas to challenge your faith?

Join us at www.hodderfaith.com, follow us on Twitter
or find us on Facebook to make sure you get the latest from
your favourite authors.

Including interviews, videos, articles, competitions
and opportunities to tell us just what you thought about
our latest releases.